The Effortless Baker

Your Complete Step-by-Step Guide to Decadent,
Showstopping Sweets and Treats

Janani Elavazhagan

Creator of Skillet To Plate

PAGE STREET
PUBLISHING CO.

PAGE STREET
PUBLISHING CO.

First published in 2023 by

Page Street Publishing Co.

27 Congress Street, Suite 1511

Salem, MA 01970

www.pagestreetpublishing.com

Distributed by Macmillan, sales in Canada by The Canadian Manda Group.

27   26   25   24   23   1   2   3   4   5

ISBN-13: 978-1-64567-812-0

ISBN-10: 1-64567-812-1

Library of Congress Control Number: 2022949768

Cover and book design by Elena Van Horn for Page Street Publishing Co.

Photography by Janani Elavazhagan

Printed and bound in the United States of America

To Amma, Mummy and Maa.

Contents

Introduction

Growing up, I was fortunate to be part of a family of great cooks who appreciated and loved good food. My grandma and mom were both excellent cooks, and their remarkable culinary skills were known to many. We used to have family gatherings with friends and relatives, and my grandma and mom would prepare an elaborate meal from appetizers to main course to desserts. Mom would effortlessly cook for up to 50 people, making it seem like an easy feat.

My father was committed to finding the best ingredients for my mother's recipes, and he would spare no effort to source them, no matter how far away they were or how time-consuming it was.

I also used to visit my grandparents in Bangalore every vacation. My grandpa, whom I fondly call Ya, was an excellent baker, and he made the most amazing sponge cake ever using a traditional oven from the 1980s. He even made his own butter at home by accumulating the cream from the milk and whisking it by hand to get a fluffy cake. I remember he used to let me whisk while he prepared the dry ingredients. He was the first baker I ever knew and my first baking inspiration.

Cooking and food have always been central to my family's culture. I started my culinary journey during my college years with a simple vegetable *khichdi* recipe taught to me by my mom. To my surprise, even my dad—a notorious food critic—was impressed with the result. This initial success ignited a passion for experimenting with different dishes, such as *gulab jamun* (which took me ten attempts to perfect). My mom was my biggest strength and supporter, standing by my side in the kitchen, sharing her own skills and nurturing me every step of the way. Thanks to her support, I didn't just try recipes—I perfected them. I enjoyed the challenge of cooking alone when my mom would encourage me to take charge during our parties.

I got married to my husband, Rakesh, after completing my bachelor's degree. When we moved to the United States, I was delighted to find a beautiful oven in our apartment kitchen. Ovens were not a common household appliance in my home country of India, and having access to one got me started baking basic recipes to hone my skills. While pursuing my master's in computer engineering, I also started a food blog, Skillet To Plate, to document my creations and share my passion for cooking. Once I had completed my degree, I shared my thought with my husband about my desire to turn my love for food into a career. He was very supportive and encouraged me to follow my dreams, despite recently graduating with a master's degree in a completely different field.

Over time, I also discovered the art of food photography and learned that a well-plated dish has a story of its own to tell. I love creating and capturing beautiful food stories and sharing my vision of food with others. This passion took on even greater meaning when I was offered the opportunity to write and photograph my own cookbook. I have always had a passion for making desserts, and my Instagram page is a testament to my love for sweets, featuring an array of mouthwatering dessert photos. So, when the chance to write a dessert cookbook presented itself, I was ecstatic beyond words!

About This Book

This cookbook blends the best of Indian and classic American desserts with the aim of making traditional Indian sweets more accessible by integrating simple baking techniques. I hope to enable everyone to savor the flavors and textures of these sweets at home.

This cookbook also features a diverse collection of American recipes and a few French classics. The recipe steps have been written in such a way so that they are approachable for new bakers. Most preparations avoid stovetop versions, and they are designed to be easy to follow and execute, allowing you to spend less time in the kitchen and more time enjoying the sweets. This book also features ten eggless recipes.

When using this book, avoid making ingredient substitutions (unless suggested or recommended) as it may affect the end result. For example, if you use melted butter or oil instead of ghee or if you substitute cake flour with all-purpose flour, I cannot guarantee the outcome. Following the recipe as written will ensure baking success. It is worth noting that most of the recipes in this book can be prepared using a hand mixer, making it a more affordable approach for home bakers who do not have the kitchen space or budget for a stand mixer.

The Effortless Baker features a delightful array of must-try desserts. The book offers you all the authentic flavors of Indian desserts, alongside beautiful food stories captured through my photography. And I've made the recipes as simple as possible, so they are perfect for bakers of all skill levels. I truly hope you enjoy this book. Happy baking!

E. Janani

Basic Techniques

Baking can be fun and challenging, and it's important to have a few basic techniques down before you start. Whether you're a beginner or an experienced baker, there are a few things to keep in mind that can make all the difference in your baking results.

Read the recipe before you begin. The first and most important technique is to **follow the recipe.** Read the instructions carefully, and make sure you have all the ingredients and equipment you need before you begin. Don't make substitutions or leave out ingredients unless otherwise suggested.

Measure your ingredients correctly. It's important to measure your ingredients accurately to ensure the best results. Always use the correct measuring tools and techniques. When measuring flour, don't pack the flour into the cup, as this can result in too much flour and a dry or tough baked good. Be sure to measure your flour properly by spooning it into your measuring cup and leveling it off with a knife. For liquids, use a liquid measuring cup that allows you to see the measurement at eye level.

Pay attention to the ingredients. Many recipes call for ingredients to be brought to room temperature before using. This is especially important for butter, eggs and dairy products, such as cream cheese. Room-temperature ingredients mix together more easily, resulting in a smoother, more consistent batter or dough.

Bloom gelatin before using it in a recipe. It's important to bloom gelatin by soaking it in cold water for a few minutes, until it softens and absorbs water. This helps it dissolve more easily and evenly when it is added to a recipe.

Pay attention to mixing, beating and scraping. When mixing your batter, be careful **not to overmix.** This can cause your baked goods to become tough and dry. Scrape down the sides of the bowl regularly to ensure all ingredients are fully incorporated. When it comes to beating egg whites, use a clean, dry bowl and beaters—and be patient. It can take several minutes to achieve the desired volume and stiffness.

Chill the bowl and beaters before you make whipped cream. Creating a colder environment for the cream helps it to whip up faster and hold its shape better. By using this technique, you can ensure that your whipped cream is light, fluffy and stable, and it will be perfect for topping cakes, pies or any other dessert that calls for it.

Line the pan with parchment paper. Cut a piece of parchment paper to fit the bottom of the baking pan. Grease the bottom and sides of the pan, then place the parchment paper in the bottom and press down. You can also cut strips of parchment paper to line the sides of the pan, leaving a little extra height to make it easier to remove whatever you are making from the pan.

Finally, have fun baking! Remember, baking should be an enjoyable experience. Don't be discouraged if your final product doesn't turn out perfectly. Making mistakes is a natural part of learning—and with each attempt, you'll gain valuable knowledge and improve your skills. So, keep trying and don't give up! Just have fun and enjoy the process.

Ingredients & What I Use

Butter & Oil

Butter is the commonly used ingredient in baking, adding flavor and richness to recipes. Its temperature is an important factor, and room-temperature or softened butter is ideal for most recipes. In my baking, I always opt for unsalted butter that is organic and grassfed. I enjoy using extra virgin olive oil for its rich and complex flavor, while grapeseed or sunflower oil are better suited for recipes that require a more neutral flavor.

Eggs

Eggs are an essential ingredient in baking, serving as a binder while also adding structure, richness and airiness to the texture of the final product. I always use organic, free-range large eggs in my recipes. It's best to let the eggs sit on the counter for at least 30 minutes so that they are at room temperature prior to preparing the batter to ensure even mixing and proper emulsification. If a recipe calls for separating the yolks and egg white, an egg separator can be a useful tool for easy separation. You can easily find egg separators online, including on Amazon.

Cardamom Powder

Cardamom is a spice that is used commonly in Indian cooking and baking. It is aromatic, and it adds a warm, sweet flavor to dishes. A lot of recipes in this book are cardamom flavored. It's best and economical to buy whole cardamom pods and blend them along with sugar to make a fine powder. Please refer to page 188 for instructions on how to make your own cardamom powder.

Chocolate & Cocoa Powder

Chocolate is a versatile ingredient that is used in cakes, brownies, cookies and more. Most recipes in this book call for bittersweet or semisweet chocolate, for its rich, deep flavor; I always use Ghirardelli® or Scharffen Berger™. Cocoa powder is used in baking to add chocolate flavor to recipes. There are two types of cocoa powder: natural and Dutch process. Natural cocoa powder is more acidic and bitter. Most recipes in this book use Dutch process cocoa powder, for its smoother and milder chocolate flavor and my favorite is Rodelle®.

Flour

Cake flour has a lower protein content than all-purpose flour, resulting in a more tender and delicate texture, making it ideal for cakes and pastries. I do not recommend substituting cake flour with all-purpose flour. I use Softasilk® or King Arthur Baking Company® unbleached cake flour for my cakes. All-purpose flour has a moderate protein content, making it a good choice for a wide variety of recipes including chocolate cakes and banana breads. I always use King Arthur. Bread flour, on the other hand, has a higher protein content than all-purpose flour. This makes it ideal for recipes that require a lot of structure, such as bread or pâte à choux. I also prefer the King Arthur brand for bread flour.

Gelatin

Gelatin is a protein-based ingredient used to create a variety of desserts, such as mousses, panna cottas and jellies. The recipes in this book use gelatin powder and my go-to brand is Knox®. You could substitute it with agar-agar for a vegan option.

Ghee

Ghee is a type of clarified butter commonly used in Indian cooking. Ghee is made by simmering butter and then removing the milk solids, leaving a pure butterfat. It has a higher smoke point and longer shelf life than regular butter, and adds a rich and nutty flavor to baked goods. All my Indian-flavored desserts use ghee for that authentic taste. You can make your own ghee at home (page 190) or you can purchase Nanak™ ghee, which I highly recommend. It's important to store ghee in a dark place at room temperature and avoid substituting it with butter, as the flavor and texture will differ.

Heavy Whipping Cream or Heavy Cream

Heavy whipping cream adds richness to desserts such as panna cotta and can be whipped into soft or stiff peaks for frosting or filling cakes. It is commonly found in grocery stores on the dairy aisle. I always use organic, pasteurized heavy whipping cream with a fat content of at least 40% in my baking. It is commonly called double cream in the U.K.

Khova (Mawa)

Khova, or *mawa*, is a popular dairy product used in many Indian sweets and desserts due to its slightly sweet and nutty flavor. It is made by slowly simmering milk, until it thickens to a fudge-like consistency. This process requires constant stirring to prevent scorching. This book features a few recipes that require khova, which can be made in the microwave for a quick and effortless process. See page 191 for instructions for making homemade khova.

Leaveners

Leaveners are ingredients that help baked goods to rise and become light and fluffy. The most common are baking powder, baking soda and cream of tartar. It's recommended to use aluminum-free baking powder, such as Rumford®, and ensure that the leaveners are fresh and not more than three months old. Refrigerating them can help maintain their freshness.

Mascarpone & Ricotta Cheese

Mascarpone is a rich, creamy cheese that is commonly used in Italian desserts such as tiramisu and cheesecake. My go-to brands are BelGioioso® or Galbani®. This cheese is very delicate, so it's important to use cold mascarpone cheese straight from the refrigerator and its best to avoid overbeating as this can cause the cheese to curdle. Ricotta cheese is a versatile ingredient in baking, with a soft texture and a mild flavor. It is very similar to paneer, which is an Indian cottage cheese. I prefer to use Galbani whole-milk ricotta cheese in all my recipes.

Sour Cream & Buttermilk

Sour cream has a tangy flavor and a creamy texture that adds richness and moisture to baked goods. I always use full-fat sour cream, though it can be substituted with plain unsweetened Greek yogurt. In baking, buttermilk often is used as a leavening agent. It helps the baked goods rise when combined with baking soda and create a tender, moist texture. Buttermilk can be found in most grocery stores, or it can be made at home by adding 1 tablespoon (15 ml) of vinegar or lemon juice to 1 cup (240 ml) of milk and allowing it to sit for a few minutes, or until it curdles. Plain, unsweetened kefir is a wonderful substitute to buttermilk.

Sweeteners

In baking, granulated sugar is a widely used sweetener that often is creamed with butter to create a light and airy texture in cakes and cookies. Brown sugar, both light and dark, is also used commonly in baking to add richness, moisture and depth of flavor to certain desserts, such as my Sticky Toffee Pudding (page 53) or Cardamom-Pecan-Pumpkin Layer Cake (page 91). For my baking needs, I prefer to use Wholesome® brand for both white and brown sugar. Jaggery is an unrefined sugar with a distinctive taste of caramel and molasses. It often is used in traditional Indian desserts, and it can be found in solid or powdered form at Indian grocery stores or online. Confectioners' sugar, also known as powdered or icing sugar, is a finely ground sugar with a small amount of added cornstarch. It's often used for frosting, meringues and glazes.

Saffron

Saffron is derived from the flower of the *Crocus sativus* plant. It has a distinct flavor and aroma and is commonly used in Indian desserts. Saffron strands are most often steeped in warm milk or water to extract the amazing flavor and beautiful color (though sometimes they are also crushed in a mortar and pestle), which is then used in the recipe. It can be quite expensive, but a little goes a long way. My favorite brands are Zaran™ and Bell Saffron®, and they are easily found at online retailers.

Vanilla Bean, Vanilla Extract & Other Flavorings

Vanilla beans are a popular ingredient used to impart a rich and complex flavor. To use a vanilla bean, simply slice the bean lengthwise and scrape out the seeds with the back of a knife. The seeds can be added directly to the recipe, or they can be steeped in a liquid to infuse the flavor. I always use Nielsen-Massey®, Rodelle, Taylor & Colledge® or Amoretti® extracts for added depth.

SIMPLE EVERYDAY
CAKES & SWEETS

From Bundt cakes to one-bowl cakes to tres leches, this chapter covers a variety of sweet treats that are perfect for any occasion. Whether you're looking for a classic American cake, such as chiffon (page 21) or chocolate sheet cake (page 45), or a unique Indian dessert, such as Makkan Peda Cake (page 35) or Ricotta Rasmalai Tres Leches (page 32), this chapter has it all. The Carrot Halwa Cake with Ricotta Malai Frosting (page 41) and the Badam Paal Crème Brûlée (page 59) also are noteworthy options that offer exotic twists to traditional cake flavors.

This section also includes a range of beautiful fall desserts that are perfect for the season. The Apple Tahini Cake (page 38) is deliciously moist, and it's perfect for a cozy fall evening. The Sticky Toffee Pudding (page 53) is a classic British dessert that is sure to satisfy any sweet tooth. And the Pumpkin-Chocolate Marble Loaf Cake (page 50) is a perfect fusion of American flavors with a touch of seasonal pumpkin spice. Each has a unique flavor profile that will leave you craving more.

White Chocolate–Raspberry Bundt Cake

♣ Makes 1 Bundt cake ♣

Whether it is a birthday, anniversary or any other special occasion, this easy and delicious cake is a family favorite. It is made using a combination of white chocolate, raspberries and a rich cake batter, and it comes together in a beautiful Bundt shape to create a visually stunning cake that tastes just as good as it looks. The tartness of the raspberries pairs perfectly with the sweetness of the white chocolate, and the tangy cream cheese glaze drizzled all over is sure to impress any dessert lover!

Cake

2 tbsp (25 g) shortening, for the pan

2½ cups (300 g) cake flour, plus more for dusting the pan (page 191 or store-bought)

1 cup (168 g) white chocolate chips (preferably Ghirardelli)

¾ cup (168 g) unsalted butter, softened

¾ cup (180 ml) olive, avocado or grapeseed oil

½ cup (34 g) nonfat dry milk powder

2 tsp (9 g) baking powder

1 tsp salt

5 large eggs, at room temperature

1 cup (240 ml) sour cream, at room temperature

1½ cups (300 g) granulated sugar

1 tbsp (15 ml) good-quality pure vanilla extract

½ tsp almond extract

½ tsp lemon extract

1 cup (125 g) fresh raspberries, pureed and strained

Prepare to bake. Preheat the oven to 325°F (165°C) with a rack in the middle. Grease a 10- to 12-cup (2.4- to 2.8-L) Bundt pan with melted shortening, which can be melted in the microwave and used immediately without cooling. Use a silicone pastry brush to ensure all creases of the Bundt pan are covered in shortening, then dust the pan with 1 to 2 tablespoons (8 to 16 g) of flour.

Next, melt the chocolate chips and butter. Microwave the white chocolate chips and butter in a medium, microwave-safe bowl at medium power (50%) for 30 to 60 seconds, or until the chocolate has melted, stirring every 20 to 30 seconds. Once the chocolate has melted completely, whisk in the oil. Set it aside to cool completely (*white chocolate mixture*).

Mix the dry ingredients. In a medium bowl, whisk together the cake flour, milk powder, baking powder and salt (*dry ingredients*) until combined.

Make the white chocolate cake batter. In a large mixing bowl, whisk the eggs until pale. Add the sour cream and sugar, whisking until well combined. Gently whisk in the dry ingredients, white chocolate mixture, vanilla, almond extract and lemon extract until the batter is smooth and free of lumps. Be careful not to over-whisk the batter (*white chocolate cake batter*).

Make the raspberry cake batter. Take ½ cup (120 ml) of the white chocolate cake batter and mix it with the raspberry puree (*raspberry cake batter*).

(continued)

White Chocolate–Raspberry Bundt Cake (continued)

Cream Cheese Glaze

4 oz (113 g) cream cheese, at room temperature

1 cup (120 g) confectioners' sugar

A pinch of salt

1 tsp vanilla extract

6 tbsp (90 ml) whole milk

Bake the cake. Pour half the white chocolate cake batter into the prepared Bundt pan. **Next,** spoon the raspberry cake batter on top of the white chocolate batter. **Then,** spoon the remaining white chocolate cake batter on top of the raspberry cake batter. Gently tap the pan on the surface and bake for 50 to 60 minutes, or until a cake skewer or toothpick inserted into the center comes out clean. Once baked, let the cake cool in the pan for 1 minute; don't leave it any longer or it may stick. Slice off any cake dome with a serrated knife. Invert the Bundt pan onto a cooling rack and allow the cake to cool completely.

Make the cream cheese glaze. Beat the cream cheese, confectioners' sugar and salt with an electric mixer until well combined. **Then,** add the vanilla and milk and beat until the glaze is smooth. Drizzle the mixture over the cooled Bundt cake.

Brown Butter–Vanilla Pound Cake

♠ Makes one 9 × 5–inch (23 × 13–cm) loaf cake ♠

This cake is made with a rich, moist pound cake batter that is infused with the nutty and toasty flavor of brown butter. The flavor and aroma of brown butter reminds me of fresh ghee, which my mom used to make at home. I've used the microwave to make the brown butter to make the process effortless and less intimidating than the stovetop version. Once the cake is baked and cooled, it is sliced and drizzled generously with bourbon butterscotch sauce. The richness of the brown butter pairs perfectly with the warmth of the bourbon and the sweetness of the sauce. The moist, tender crumb of the pound cake makes it a wonderful treat to enjoy with a cup of coffee or tea.

Cake

2 tbsp (28 g) unsalted butter, for the pan

1 cup (225 g) unsalted butter, softened

2 cups (250 g) all-purpose flour

1 tsp baking powder

½ tsp salt

Prepare to bake. Preheat the oven to 325°F (165°C) with a rack in the middle. Using a silicone pastry brush, coat a 9 × 5–inch (23 × 13–cm) loaf pan with melted butter, which can be melted in the microwave and used immediately without cooling. Line the bottom of the pan with parchment paper, leaving some paper hanging over the sides of the pan for easy removal of the loaf.

Make the brown butter. In a 4-quart (3.8-L) microwave-safe bowl, place ½ cup (112 g) of the butter and cover it with a microwave-safe plate that fits properly. This step is important as the butter may splash and splatter during the process. Microwave the butter in 30-second intervals for 5 to 8 minutes, stirring every 30 seconds. Keep a close eye on it as it browns. You'll know it's ready when it emits a nutty aroma and turns a dark amber color. Using oven mitts, carefully remove the bowl from the microwave. Transfer the brown butter to another bowl and set it aside to cool completely. Repeat the same process with the remaining ½ cup (112 g) of butter. Once this batch turns dark amber in color, carefully add it to the previous batch and set all of the brown butter aside to cool completely. By browning the butter in smaller batches, you can avoid making a mess in the microwave. Take care while working with the hot butter and ensure it has cooled before using it in your recipe.

Sift the dry ingredients. In a medium bowl, sift the flour, baking powder and salt *(dry ingredients)*.

(continued)

Brown Butter–Vanilla Pound Cake (continued)

Cake (continued)

¼ cup (60 ml) grapeseed or vegetable oil

1½ cups (300 g) granulated sugar

3 large eggs, at room temperature

1 tbsp (15 ml) good-quality pure vanilla extract

¼ tsp almond extract

½ cup (120 ml) whole milk

Butterscotch Sauce

5 tbsp (70 g) unsalted butter

1½ cups (340 g) packed dark brown sugar

1½ cups (360 ml) heavy cream

1 tsp good-quality pure vanilla extract

½ tsp rose salt

1 tsp bourbon (optional)

Beat the fats and sugar. Using a hand mixer or a stand mixer fitted with a paddle attachment, cream the cooled brown butter, oil and sugar for 3 minutes. Scrape down the sides and the bottom of the bowl with a rubber spatula as needed. Add the eggs one at a time, beating well after each addition, scraping down the sides and the bottom of the bowl with a rubber spatula. Stir in the vanilla and the almond extract and beat until well mixed.

Combine the dry and wet ingredients. With the mixer on low speed, stir in half the dry ingredients and mix until just combined. Add the milk and mix. Add the remaining half of the dry ingredients and mix until just combined but no streaks of flour are visible.

Bake the cake. Scrape the cake batter into the prepared loaf pan and bake for 50 to 60 minutes. Tent it with aluminum foil if it browns too quickly; this will extend the baking time by 10 minutes. The cake is done when a cake skewer or toothpick inserted into the center comes out clean. Let the cake cool in the pan for 10 minutes before removing it to a cooling rack to cool completely.

Make the butterscotch sauce. Add the butter to a 4-cup (960-ml) microwave-safe measuring cup and microwave for 30-second intervals, until the butter is fully melted. **Now,** add the brown sugar and heavy cream to the melted butter. Give it a quick mix. Microwave for 3 minutes, stirring every 30 seconds. The butterscotch sauce will be bubbly and have a thin consistency after 3 minutes. Add the vanilla, rose salt and bourbon (if using) and give it a quick whisk.

Set the sauce aside to cool completely. It will thicken as it cools down. Spoon the sauce over the cake and store any leftover sauce in an airtight container in the refrigerator for up to 2 weeks.

Olive Oil Chiffon Cake

♣ Makes one 10-inch (26-cm) cake ♣

This is a delightful dessert that is light, airy and infused with the rich and fruity flavor of extra virgin olive oil. The whipped egg whites give the cake a soft and pillowy texture while the addition of olive oil keeps it moist. This cake can be enjoyed on its own or with a variety of toppings such as fresh berries or whipped cream. Its delicate texture and subtle flavor make it a perfect pairing for a variety of beverages, from coffee to tea and even a glass of wine.

2 cups (240 g) cake flour (page 191 or store-bought)

1¾ cups (350 g) granulated sugar, divided

1 tsp salt

2 tsp (9 g) baking powder

¾ cup (180 ml) extra virgin olive oil

8 large eggs, at room temperature, separated

1 tbsp (15 ml) good-quality pure vanilla extract

½ tsp almond extract

½ tsp lemon extract

½ cup (120 ml) whole milk

½ tsp cream of tartar

Confectioners' sugar, for dusting (optional)

Tip

If you are using a tube pan that does not have feet, you'll need to keep the pan elevated while it cools upside down. One way to do this is to place the tube pan over a bottle or similar object with a narrow neck, and let it cool for at least 1 hour in this position. This will prevent the cake from collapsing as it cools and ensure that it retains its light and airy texture.

Prepare to bake. Preheat the oven to 325°F (165°C) with a rack in the middle. Line the bottom of a 10-inch (26-cm) footed angel food pan (see Tip) with parchment paper. Do not grease the pan.

Mix the ingredients. First, whisk together the cake flour, 1¼ cups (250 g) of sugar, salt, and baking powder *(dry ingredients)* in a medium bowl until combined. **Then,** in a small bowl, whisk together the oil, egg yolks, vanilla, almond extract, lemon extract and milk *(wet ingredients)* until well combined. **Finally,** pour the wet ingredients into the dry ingredients. Whisk together the batter until it is well mixed *(wet batter)*.

Beat the egg whites. In a large clean bowl, using a hand mixer or a stand mixer fitted with a whisk attachment, beat the egg whites with the cream of tartar for about 2 minutes, until medium peaks form. Gradually add ½ cup (100 g) of sugar while continuing to beat on high speed for 1 to 2 minutes, or until glossy, stiff peaks form.

Fold in the egg whites and bake the cake. To avoid the deflation of the egg whites, gently fold in the egg whites in three batches using the cut-and-fold method. The egg whites should be folded very gently and fully mixed with the wet batter. Spoon the batter into the prepared pan and bake for 50 to 65 minutes, or until a cake skewer or toothpick inserted into the center comes out clean. Remove it from the oven and set it upside down to cool for 1 hour.

Finish the cake. The cake should fall off the pan after a few gentle shakes. If it doesn't, run an offset spatula around the edges to remove the cake from the pan. Dust the cake with confectioners' sugar (if using). Store leftover chiffon cake covered in an airtight container. It will keep at room temperature for 2 to 3 days or in the fridge for up to 1 week. It also freezes well for up to 2 months.

Brown Butter, Cardamom & Banana Bundt Cake

♠ Makes 1 large Bundt cake ♠

This cake is a perfect fall dessert that combines rich, warm flavors and a luscious, salted caramel sauce. The cake is made with ripe bananas, fragrant cardamom and nutty brown butter, all combined to create a tender crumb. It blends the aromatic flavors of South Indian cuisine with a classic American baked treat and is sure to please anyone who loves rich, comforting flavors. And, of course, the brown butter is made effortlessly in the microwave, taking the intimidation factor out of the recipe.

Cake

2 tbsp (25 g) shortening, for the pan

3 cups (375 g) all-purpose flour, plus more for the pan and walnuts

½ cup (60 g) walnuts, chopped

½ cup (112 g) unsalted butter, softened

2 tsp (9 g) baking powder

1 tsp baking soda

1 tsp salt

1 tbsp (7 g) cardamom powder (page 188 or store-bought)

Prepare to bake. Preheat the oven to 325°F (165°C) with a rack in the middle. Thoroughly grease a 10- to 12-cup (2.4- to 2.8-L) Bundt pan with melted shortening, which can be melted in the microwave and used immediately without cooling. Use a silicone pastry brush to ensure all creases of the Bundt pan are covered in butter, then dust the pan with 1 tablespoon (8 g) of flour. Toss the walnuts in 2 teaspoons (5 g) of flour. Set them aside.

Make the brown butter. In a 4-quart (3.8-L) microwave-safe bowl, place the butter and cover it with a microwave-safe plate that fits properly. This step is important as the butter may splash and splatter during the process. Microwave the butter in 30-second intervals for 5 to 8 minutes, stirring every 30 seconds. Keep a close eye on it as it browns. You'll know it's ready when it emits a nutty aroma and turns a dark amber color. Using oven mitts, carefully remove the bowl from the microwave. Transfer the brown butter to another bowl and set it aside to cool completely.

Mix the dry ingredients. In a medium bowl, whisk together the flour, baking powder, baking soda, salt and cardamom *(dry ingredients)*.

(continued)

Cake (continued)

¼ cup (60 ml) olive oil

1 cup (200 g) granulated sugar

1 cup (225 g) packed dark
brown sugar

4 large eggs, at room temperature

2 cups (450 g) mashed banana
(very ripe)

1 cup (240 ml) sour cream or
yogurt, at room temperature

1 tbsp (15 ml) good-quality pure
vanilla extract

Salted Caramel Sauce

2 cups (400 g) granulated sugar

6 tbsp (84 g) unsalted butter,
softened

1¼ cups (300 ml) heavy cream, at
room temperature

1½ tbsp (25 g) rose salt

1 tsp good-quality pure vanilla
extract

Beat the fats and sugar and add all the wet ingredients. Using a hand mixer or a stand mixer fitted with a paddle attachment, beat the brown butter, oil, granulated sugar and brown sugar for 2 minutes. Scrape down the sides and the bottom of the bowl with a rubber spatula as needed. Add the eggs one at a time, beating well after each addition, scraping down the sides and the bottom of the bowl with a rubber spatula. **Then,** add the banana, sour cream and vanilla and beat until it's all well mixed.

Add all the dry ingredients and fold in the walnuts. With the mixer on low speed, add all the dry ingredients and mix until just combined and with no streaks of flour visible. Fold in the flour-coated walnuts.

Bake the cake. Scrape the cake batter into the prepared Bundt pan and bake for 60 to 70 minutes. The cake is done when a cake skewer or toothpick inserted into the center comes out clean. Once baked, let the cake cool in the pan for 1 minute; don't leave it any longer or it may stick. Remove any cake dome with a serrated knife. With oven mitts, invert the Bundt pan onto a cooling rack and allow the cake to cool completely.

Make the salted caramel sauce. Place the sugar in a medium, heavy-bottomed saucepan over medium heat. Stir it constantly until it melts and turns into an amber-colored liquid. Once the sugar has melted completely, add the butter and stir until it's fully incorporated. Be careful as the caramel may start to bubble rapidly, so use gloves for safety. Gradually pour in the heavy cream and mix well. Let it simmer for 30 seconds. Remove the pan from the heat and add the salt and vanilla. Stir well and set it aside to cool completely.

Serve the Bundt cake. Drizzle the caramel sauce over the cake. Any leftover caramel sauce can be stored in an airtight container in the refrigerator for up to 1 week.

Double Chocolate Fudge Bundt Cake

This double chocolate fudge Bundt cake with chocolate ganache is a decadent dessert that is sure to satisfy any chocolate lover's cravings. This cake is rich, moist and deeply chocolatey, with a smooth, silky chocolate ganache drizzled over the top. It's extremely easy to bake—and trust me, one slice won't be enough! What's more, you won't need any special equipment to whip up this delicious dessert. A whisk and spatula will do.

Cake

2 tbsp (25 g) shortening, for the pan

¾ cup (65 g) plus 2 tbsp (12 g) Dutch process cocoa powder, divided

4 oz (113 g) good-quality bittersweet chocolate, chopped (preferably Ghirardelli)

1 cup (226 g) unsalted butter, at room temperature

4 large eggs, at room temperature

1 tbsp (15 ml) good-quality pure vanilla extract

½ cup (120 ml) sour cream or plain Greek yogurt, at room temperature

3 tbsp (45 ml) olive, avocado, vegetable or canola oil

2 cups (250 g) all-purpose flour

2 cups (400 g) granulated sugar

1 tsp espresso powder

½ tsp kosher salt

1 tsp baking powder

¼ tsp baking soda

Prepare to bake. Preheat the oven to 325°F (165°C) with a rack in the middle. Thoroughly grease a 10- to 12-cup (2.4- to 2.8-L) Bundt cake pan with melted shortening, which can be melted in the microwave and used immediately without cooling. Use a silicone pastry brush to ensure all creases of the Bundt pan are covered in shortening, then dust the pan with 2 tablespoons (12 g) of cocoa powder.

Melt the chocolate and butter. In a large, microwave-safe bowl, add the chocolate and heat it in the microwave oven at medium power (50%) for 60 to 90 seconds. Stir it every 20 to 30 seconds, until the chocolate has fully melted. **Next,** slice the softened butter and add it to the melted chocolate. Mix well using a spatula until the butter is fully melted and combined with the chocolate. Once the chocolate and butter have melted, add the ¾ cup (65 g) of cocoa powder and stir until everything is well combined. Set the mixture aside to cool *(chocolate mixture)*.

Mix the ingredients. First, in a small bowl or a glass measuring cup, combine the eggs, vanilla, sour cream and oil. Beat the mixture using a fork and set it aside *(egg mixture)*. **Then,** add the flour, sugar, espresso powder, salt, baking powder and baking soda into the cooled chocolate mixture using a spatula *(flour-chocolate mixture)*. **Finally,** using a balloon whisk, gently fold the egg mixture into the flour-chocolate mixture until well mixed *(batter)*.

Bake the cake. Scrape the batter into the prepared Bundt pan and bake for 50 to 60 minutes, or until a cake skewer or toothpick inserted into the center comes out clean. Remove the cake from the oven and let it cool in the pan for 30 seconds. Be careful not to let it cool for too long, as this could cause the cake to stick to the pan. Remove any cake dome with a serrated knife. Using oven mitts, invert the Bundt pan onto a cooling rack and let the cake cool completely.

(continued)

Double Chocolate Fudge Bundt Cake (continued)

Ganache

¾ cup (180 ml) heavy cream

½ cup (84 g) good-quality bittersweet or semisweet chocolate chips (preferably Ghirardelli)

Make the ganache. In a 4-cup (960-ml) microwave-safe glass measuring cup, heat the heavy cream for 45 to 60 seconds, or until it just starts to bubble around the edges. Then, add the chocolate chips to a small bowl and pour the hot cream over the chips. Stir until everything is well combined. Spoon the ganache over the cake and store any leftover cake in an airtight container at room temperature for up to 2 days or up to 1 week in refrigerator. This cake also freezes well for a month or two.

Ricotta–Olive Oil Almond Cake with Summer Fruits

♠ Makes one 9-inch (23-cm) cake ♣

One of my favorite summertime activities is picking fruit, and when it comes to choosing a cake to bake during the season, this rustic olive oil ricotta cake is my top choice. I love this cake for its simplicity and versatility. The cake is made with a combination of ricotta cheese and olive oil, which gives it a tender and moist texture. The addition of almond flour adds a nutty and slightly sweet flavor, complementing the richness of the ricotta cheese and the fruity notes of the olive oil. The use of fresh summer fruits adds a natural sweetness, which is both light and refreshing. When serving the cake, you can either sprinkle confectioners' sugar over it or pair it with a scoop of creamy vanilla ice cream for an even more delicious dessert.

1½ cups (180 g) cake flour (page 191 or store-bought)

1 cup (104 g) almond flour

1¾ cups (350 g) granulated sugar

2 tsp (9 g) baking powder

½ tsp salt

½ cup (120 ml) olive oil

3 large eggs, at room temperature

1 tbsp (15 ml) good-quality pure vanilla extract

15 oz (425 g) whole-milk ricotta cheese, at room temperature (see Tips)

2 large peaches, peeled, pit removed and chopped (see Tips)

Confectioners' sugar, for dusting (optional)

Prepare to bake. Preheat the oven to 350°F (175°C) with a rack in the middle. Spray a 9-inch (23-cm) round pan with nonstick spray and line the bottom of the pan with parchment paper.

Mix the ingredients. Combine the cake flour, almond flour, sugar, baking powder and salt in a large bowl *(dry ingredients)*. Make a well in the center and add the oil, eggs, vanilla and cheese. Use a whisk to gently combine all the ingredients until everything is well mixed.

Fold in the peaches and bake the cake. Fold the peaches into the batter and gently mix until combined. Spoon the batter into the prepared pan and bake for 50 to 65 minutes, or until a cake skewer or toothpick inserted into the center comes out clean. Let the cake cool in the pan for 5 minutes before inverting onto a cooling rack. Once the cake is at room temperature, dust it with confectioners' sugar (if using) and top it with fresh fruits. Store the cake in the refrigerator for 4 to 7 days or freeze for up to 1 month.

Tips

You can replace peaches with figs or any summer fruits.

I highly recommend using whole-milk ricotta for the best tasting cake.

Baked Fragrant Rice Kheer

♣ Makes 6 to 8 servings ♣

Kheer is a traditional Indian dessert that is typically made on the stovetop by slow cooking rice in a mixture of milk and sugar. Here you have a recipe for baked kheer, which is an excellent way to enjoy the classic dessert without putting in a lot of effort. To make it even more indulgent, it is served with a perfect complement to the flavors of the kheer—pears baked in sugar syrup with cardamom, until they are soft and tender. The sprinkle of saffron adds a beautiful golden hue to the pears. With its creamy texture, fragrant spices and deliciously sweet flavor, this is sure to become a favorite among dessert lovers.

Rice Kheer

1 cup (197 g) arborio rice, washed and rinsed

2 cups (475 ml) canned coconut milk

2 cups (475 ml) whole milk

1 cup (240 ml) water

½ cup (100 g) granulated sugar

¼ cup (31 g) crushed raw pistachios

1 tbsp (7 g) cardamom powder (page 188 or store-bought)

2 tbsp (26 g) ghee (page 190 or store-bought)

1 vanilla bean

Baked Saffron Pears

½ cup (100 g) granulated sugar

1 cup (240 ml) water

1 tsp cardamom powder (page 188 or store-bought)

¼ tsp saffron strands

2 pears, stemmed and cored and cut into 8 slices each

For Serving (optional)

½ cup (120 ml) whole milk

Chopped nuts

Bake the rice kheer. Preheat the oven to 300°F (150°C) with a rack in the middle. Grab a 3-quart (2.8-L) baking pan. Add the rice, coconut milk, whole milk, water, sugar, pistachios, cardamom and ghee *(kheer mixture)* to the pan. Split the vanilla bean and scrape the seeds into the mixture, then add the pod as well. Mix the ingredients using a fork to combine. Bake for 1 hour 35 minutes to 1 hour 45 minutes, or until the rice is fully cooked and a golden skin has formed. Once it's done, take the pan out of the oven and let it cool to room temperature. **Finally,** chill it in the refrigerator until you're ready to serve.

Bake the saffron pears. Preheat the oven to 400°F (200°C). Prepare the saffron syrup by mixing the sugar, water, cardamom and saffron in a 4-cup (960-ml) microwave-safe measuring cup. Microwave the mixture on high for 1 to 2 minutes, or until the sugar dissolves completely. Take a 1¼-quart (1.2-L) baking dish and place the sliced pears in it, cut side up. Pour the saffron syrup over the pears and bake them in the oven for 30 minutes. **Then,** turn the pears cut side down and spoon the saffron syrup over the top. Bake for 20 to 50 minutes, or until the pears become soft.

Serve the baked coconut milk rice kheer. To serve, transfer the rice pudding to a serving plate. If you prefer a thinner consistency, add some milk to adjust the thickness. Top the pudding with a slice of baked pear and drizzle some saffron syrup over it. **Finally,** sprinkle some nuts on top for garnish (if using).

Ricotta Rasmalai Tres Leches

♣ Makes one 9 × 13–inch (23 × 33–cm) sheet cake ♣

Here you have a delightful dessert that combines the traditional Indian dessert of *rasmalai* with the Latin American tres leches cake. This fusion dessert is an excellent representation of how diverse food cultures can come together to create something unique and delicious. Rasmalai is a classic Indian dessert made from paneer (cottage cheese) dumplings soaked in saffron-flavored milk. Tres leches cake is a sponge cake soaked in a mixture of three types of milk: condensed milk, evaporated milk and heavy cream. The combination of the two creates a light and spongy cake with a hint of Indian flavors. This version is made with ricotta cheese instead of paneer, which gives the cake a lighter and fluffier texture. The cake is soaked in *rabdi*, a thick and creamy Indian dessert made by simmering milk on low heat until it thickens, then flavoring it with cardamom and saffron. I've made the method for making rabdi much easier by using the microwave exclusively. When adding saffron to the recipe, don't be afraid to add more, as it brings out the authentic rasmalai flavor in every bite. Trust me, you won't regret it!

Cake

1 tbsp (15 ml) melted butter, for the pan

1 cup (240 ml) whole milk

¼ tsp saffron strands (see Tips)

2½ cups (300 g) cake flour (page 191 or store-bought)

½ tsp baking soda

1 tsp baking powder

1 tsp cardamom powder (page 188 or store-bought)

1½ cups (300 g) granulated sugar

⅛ tsp salt

1 cup (250 g) whole-milk ricotta, at room temperature

½ cup (120 ml) vegetable oil

Rabdi

2 cups (475 ml) whole milk

1 cup (240 ml) sweetened condensed milk

1 cup (240 ml) heavy whipping cream

½ tsp saffron strands

1 tsp cardamom powder (page 188 or store-bought)

Prepare to bake. Preheat the oven to 350°F (175°C) with a rack in the middle. Line a 9 × 13–inch (23 × 33–cm) pan with parchment paper and lightly brush with the melted butter using a silicone pastry brush and set it aside.

Make the saffron milk. In a 4-cup (960-ml) microwave-safe measuring cup, heat the milk along with saffron strands for 1 to 2 minutes, until it reaches just a boil. Allow it to cool completely (*saffron milk*).

Mix the ingredients. First, in a large bowl, whisk together the cake flour, baking soda, baking powder, cardamom, sugar and salt (*dry ingredients*) until combined. **Next,** in a small bowl, use a fork to whisk the ricotta cheese and set it aside (*ricotta cheese*). **Finally,** add the saffron milk, oil and ricotta cheese to the dry ingredients. Gently whisk together until it's well combined and there are no visible lumps. Be careful not to overmix the batter at this stage.

Bake the cake. Scrape the batter into the prepared pan and bake for 20 to 30 minutes, or until a cake skewer or toothpick inserted into the center comes out clean.

Make the rabdi mixture. While the cake bakes, combine the whole milk, sweetened condensed milk, heavy whipping cream, saffron and cardamom in a large, microwave-safe bowl. Whisk the mixture and microwave it for 2 to 3 minutes, until it reaches a boil. Allow the rabdi mixture to cool completely.

(continued)

Ricotta Rasmalai Tres Leches (continued)

For Serving

Whipped cream (page 185)

Sliced raw pistachios

Tips

Make sure to include saffron in your recipe, as it adds an essential flavor to the rasmalai.

Be careful not to overmix the batter.

Pour the rabdi mixture all over the cake and set it in the refrigerator. Once the cake is finished baking, use a fork to prick it all over while it's still hot. Gradually pour three-quarters of the rabdi mixture all over the cake, tilting the pan as needed to ensure the cake fully absorbs the rabdi. Chill the cake in the refrigerator for at least 4 to 5 hours or overnight. Reserve the remaining one-quarter of the rabdi mixture for serving and store it separately in the refrigerator.

Serve the ricotta rasmalai tres leches. Transfer the cake to a serving plate and cut it into four rectangles. Use a piping bag to add the whipped cream. Sprinkle the pistachios on top, and drizzle the remaining rabdi mixture around the cake.

Makkan Peda Cake

♠ Makes six 4-inch (10-cm) cakes ♠

Makkan peda is a popular, sweet delicacy from the town of Arcot in the Indian state of Tamil Nādu. It is similar in taste to gulab jamun but richer, with a stuffing of mixed nuts and a soak in saffron syrup. This is a childhood favorite of mine, and I have created a replica of this recipe in the form of a cake. Every bite of this cake will remind you of the authentic makkan peda, and if you're a fan of gulab jamun, then you're in for a treat. Moreover, this cake recipe is eggless, staying true to the traditional gulab jamun recipe.

Khova (Mawa)

½ cup (34 g) nonfat dry milk powder

½ tsp ghee, solid room temperature (page 190 or store-bought)

¼ cup plus 2 tbsp (90 ml) heavy whipping cream

Cake

1 tbsp (15 ml) melted ghee, for the pans (page 190 or store-bought)

1¼ cups (150 g) cake flour (page 191 or store-bought)

1 tsp baking powder

¼ tsp baking soda

¼ tsp cardamom powder (page 188 or store-bought)

1 cup (200 g) granulated sugar

½ tsp salt

¼ cup (65 g) ricotta cheese, at room temperature

½ cup (120 ml) yogurt, at room temperature

½ cup (120 ml) whole milk, at room temperature

¼ cup (52 g) ghee, melted and cooled (page 190 or store-bought)

¾ cup (112 g) mixed nuts and seeds, chopped (e.g., cashews, almonds, pistachios, char magaz and charoli), tossed or coated in 2 tsp (5 g) all-purpose flour

Make the khova. Combine the milk powder, ghee and heavy cream in a large, microwave-safe bowl. Whisk until the mixture is smooth. Microwave on high in 30-second intervals, stirring every 30 seconds, until the mixture has dried up and formed a solid mass. This should not take more than 2 minutes. Once the khova is ready, allow it to cool completely.

Prepare to bake. Preheat the oven to 350°F (175°C) with a rack in the middle. Use a silicone pastry brush to generously apply ghee to six 4-inch (10-cm) cake pans, ensuring that all surfaces are covered. Line the pans with parchment paper. Place the pans on a baking sheet and set them aside.

Mix the ingredients and bake the cake. First, in a large bowl, whisk together the cake flour, baking powder, baking soda, cardamom, sugar and salt *(dry ingredients)*. In a medium bowl, whisk the ricotta cheese, yogurt, khova, and milk until they are well mixed *(wet ingredients)*. Set this mixture aside. **Then,** add the cooled ghee and wet ingredients to the dry ingredients. Gently whisk the mixture until the flour is no longer visible. Fold in the nuts coated in flour. **Next,** equally divide the batter between the prepared pans and bake for 35 to 40 minutes, until the tops are golden brown or a cake skewer or toothpick inserted into the center comes out clean. Once the cake is done, take it out of the oven, but leave it in the pan.

(continued)

Makkan Peda Cake (continued)

Saffron Sugar Syrup

1 cup (240 ml) water

½ cup (100 g) granulated sugar

½ tsp lemon juice

¼ tsp saffron

1 tsp rose water

¼ tsp cardamom powder
(page 188 or store-bought)

Make the saffron syrup. In a 4-cup (960-ml) microwave-safe measuring cup, combine the water, sugar, lemon juice, saffron, rose water and cardamom. Whisk the syrup mixture and microwave it for about 3 to 4 minutes, until it reaches a temperature of 190° to 200°F (88° to 93°C), or until the sugar is dissolved completely and the syrup is hot.

Pour the saffron syrup all over the cake. Pierce all six cakes with a fork while still warm, and reserve one-quarter of the saffron syrup. Gradually spoon three-quarters of the syrup over the cakes, dividing it evenly. Wait for 5 to 10 minutes, then use a knife to loosen the edges and flip the cakes onto a serving platter. Drizzle the remaining syrup on top when serving.

Apple Tahini Cake

♠ Makes 1 Bundt cake or a 9-inch (23-cm) cake ♣

As soon as autumn sets in, I can't help but think about heading out to pick apples for a lovely, rustic apple cake. This cake is perfect for fall, and the combination of sweet apples, nutty tahini and aromatic cardamom creates a flavor profile that is both familiar and new. Walnuts are folded into the batter and baked into the cake, adding an extra layer of texture and flavor. And to take the cake to the next level, a drizzle of maple-tahini icing brings in a touch of sweetness and creaminess. It's a great dessert for a dinner party or a potluck, as it's sure to be a crowd-pleaser.

Cake

2 tbsp (25 g) shortening, for the pan

1–2 tbsp (8–16 g) flour, for the pan

½ cup (60 g) walnuts, chopped

2 tsp (5 g) all-purpose flour, for the walnuts

3 cups (375 g) all-purpose flour

2 tsp (4 g) cardamom powder (page 188 or store-bought)

2 tsp (9 g) baking powder

½ tsp salt

1 cup (240 ml) olive, avocado or vegetable oil

½ cup (100 g) granulated sugar

2 cups (450 g) packed dark brown sugar

4 large eggs, at room temperature

1 tsp good-quality pure vanilla extract

1 cup (240 ml) fresh orange juice

¼ cup (60 g) tahini

2 small granny smith apples, peeled, cored and sliced

Tahini Glaze

½ cup (120 ml) maple syrup

2 tbsp (30 g) tahini

¼ tsp cardamom powder (page 188 or store-bought)

Prepare to bake. Preheat the oven to 350°F (175°C) with a rack in the middle. Thoroughly grease a 9- to 10-cup (2.1- to 2.4-L) Bundt pan or a 9-inch (23-cm) springform pan with melted shortening, which can be melted in the microwave and used immediately without cooling. Use a silicone pastry brush to ensure all creases of the Bundt pan are covered in shortening, then dust the pan with flour.

Toss the walnuts in flour. Sprinkle 2 teaspoons (5 g) of flour over the walnuts and toss to coat. Set aside.

Mix the ingredients. First, in a large bowl, whisk together the flour, cardamom, baking powder and salt *(dry ingredients)* until combined. **Then,** in a medium bowl, use a whisk to combine the oil, granulated sugar, brown sugar, eggs, vanilla, orange juice and tahini *(wet ingredients)*. **Finally,** combine the wet ingredients in the bowl with the dry ingredients, mixing until just combined and no streaks of flour remain. **Then,** fold in the walnuts.

Bake the cake. Place half the batter into the prepared Bundt pan. Arrange the apple slices on top of the batter and spoon the remaining batter over the apple slices. Bake the cake for 55 to 70 minutes, or until a cake skewer or toothpick inserted into the center comes out clean. Remove the cake from the oven and let it cool in the pan for 1 minute. Then, use oven mitts to invert the Bundt pan onto a cooling rack and allow the cake to cool completely.

Make the tahini glaze. Add the maple syrup, tahini and cardamom to a small bowl. Whisk together until well combined. Drizzle the mixture over the cake.

Tip

If you are not fond of cardamom, you may substitute it with cinnamon.

Carrot Halwa Cake with Ricotta Malai Frosting

♠ Makes one 9-inch (23-cm) cake ♠

Carrot halwa is a well-known and loved dessert in India. It is a delectable sweet prepared with shredded carrots, sugar, khova and ghee and flavored with cardamom. This cake is an adaptation of this decadent dessert, using the same ingredients used to make carrot halwa. Each bite is reminiscent of the original dessert, and to make it even more delicious, it is served with a rich malai frosting!

Cake

2 tbsp (30 ml) melted butter, for the pan

1½ cups (188 g) all-purpose flour

1¼ cups (130 g) almond flour

1½ cups (300 g) granulated sugar

1 cup (225 g) packed light brown sugar

1 tsp baking powder

½ tsp baking soda

1 tbsp (6 g) cardamom powder (page 188 or store-bought)

½ tsp salt

3 large eggs, at room temperature

1 tsp good-quality pure vanilla extract

½ cup (104 g) ghee, melted and cooled (page 190 or store-bought)

¾ cup (190 g) whole-milk ricotta cheese, at room temperature

½ cup (120 ml) whole milk, at room temperature

3¾ cups (413 g) shredded carrots

½ cup (68 g) dry roasted cashews, chopped

Ricotta Malai Frosting

½ cup (125 g) whole-milk ricotta cheese, at room temperature

½ cup (120 ml) condensed milk

1 cup (240 ml) heavy whipping cream, cold

2 tbsp (16 g) confectioners' sugar

Prepare to bake. To prepare the cake, preheat the oven to 350°F (175°C) with a rack in the middle. Brush melted butter over a 9-inch (23-cm) pan or 9-inch (23-cm) springform pan, using a silicone pastry brush; microwaved butter that is still warm is fine. Line the pan with parchment paper. Chill a mixing bowl and whisk/beaters in the refrigerator for the whipped ricotta frosting. It's important to keep the mixing bowl very cold to achieve the desired consistency.

Mix the ingredients. First, in a large bowl, whisk together the all-purpose flour, almond flour, granulated sugar, brown sugar, baking powder, baking soda, cardamom and salt *(dry ingredients)* until combined. **Next,** whisk together the eggs, vanilla and cooled ghee in a separate medium bowl using a fork until the ingredients are well combined *(wet ingredients)*. **Then,** in a separate small bowl, use a fork to gently whisk the ricotta cheese *(ricotta cheese)*. **Finally,** add the whisked wet ingredients, whisked ricotta cheese and milk to the dry ingredients. Gently whisk until everything is just combined.

Fold in the shredded carrots and nuts and bake the cake. Carefully fold the carrots and cashews into the batter. Spoon the batter into the prepared pan and bake for 60 to 80 minutes, or until a cake skewer or toothpick inserted into the center comes out clean. Let the cake cool in the pan for 5 minutes, then gently invert it onto a cooling rack and let it cool completely before frosting.

Make the ricotta malai frosting. Whisk together the ricotta cheese and condensed milk in a small bowl to prepare the ricotta cream. Take the chilled mixing bowl from the refrigerator and add the heavy cream and confectioners' sugar. Beat on medium speed for 1 minute and increase the speed to high for 5 to 6 minutes, until soft peaks form. Slowly drizzle in the ricotta cream and continue to beat for 1 to 2 minutes, until stiff peaks form. Spread the frosting on the cake and serve.

Pistachio-Citrus Upside-Down Cake

♠ Makes one 9-inch (23-cm) cake ♠

The vibrant citrus fruits in this delightful dessert make it a showstopper on any table. The cake is infused with the fragrant flavors of orange blossom water and cardamom to complement the sweetness of the fruits. The pistachios in the batter add a lovely nutty flavor and texture to the cake. The whole picture is a harmonious blend that is truly delicious. The best part about this cake is the gorgeous citrus topping. Slices of oranges and grapefruit are arranged on the bottom of the cake pan, creating a lovely mosaic-like pattern. When the cake is flipped over, they become a beautiful topping, making the cake visually stunning.

2 tbsp (30 ml) melted butter, for the pan

5 small to medium citrus fruits, any type (zest 2 before using)

½ cup (100 g) granulated sugar

2 tbsp (30 ml) water

1½ cups (180 g) cake flour (page 191 or store-bought)

¾ cup (93 g) raw pistachios, ground

1 tsp baking powder

½ tsp baking soda

1 tbsp (7 g) cardamom powder (page 188 or store-bought)

1 cup (200 g) granulated sugar

A generous pinch of saffron

2 tbsp (12 g) orange zest

½ tsp salt

3 large eggs, at room temperature

1 tsp orange blossom water

1 tsp pure vanilla extract

⅓ cup (80 ml) olive oil

¾ cup (180 ml) yogurt, at room temperature

Prepare to bake. Preheat the oven to 350°F (175°C) with a rack in the middle. Brush melted butter over a 9-inch (23-cm) pan using a silicone pastry brush; microwaved butter that is still warm is fine. Line the pan with parchment paper.

Prepare the citrus slices. Cut off the ends of each fruit with a sharp knife. Carefully cut away the peel along the edge of the fruit, taking care not to cut into the fruit itself. Remove as much of the white pith as possible, then slice the fruit into rounds that are about ¼ inch (6 mm) thick. Be sure to remove any seeds or remaining pith from the center. While removing the peel makes the fruit easier to eat, I personally enjoy the peel on my citrus slices. Keep in mind that leaving the peel on is optional.

Make a sugar slurry and arrange the citrus slices. Make a slurry by combining the sugar and water. Spread the slurry on the prepared pan and tilt in all directions to cover the parchment. Place the orange slices in a circular overlapping pattern over the sugar, covering the entire pan. Set it aside.

Mix the ingredients. First, in a large bowl, whisk together the cake flour, pistachios, baking powder, baking soda, cardamom, sugar, saffron, orange zest and salt *(dry ingredients)* until combined. **Then,** using a fork, whisk together the eggs, orange blossom water, vanilla, oil, and yogurt in a separate medium bowl until everything is well combined *(wet ingredients)*. **Finally,** add the wet ingredients to the dry ingredients and gently whisk together until no streaks of flour are visible.

Bake the cake. Pour the cake batter over the arranged orange slices in the prepared pan and bake for 40 to 50 minutes, or until a cake skewer or toothpick inserted into the center comes out clean. Let the cake rest in the pan for 5 to 10 minutes, then use a knife to loosen the edges if needed. Carefully invert the cake onto a serving plate and remove the parchment paper. Let the cake rest for at least 4 to 5 hours on the counter before serving.

Rich Olive Oil–Chocolate Sheet Cake

♠ Makes one 9 × 13–inch (23 × 33–cm) cake ♠

Here is a decadent dessert that is perfect for any occasion. The combination of rich chocolate and the fruity notes of olive oil makes this cake an unforgettable treat. This cake is incredibly easy to make, as it is a sheet cake that can be baked and served in the same pan. It's perfect for a crowd, making it a great option for parties or family gatherings. The frosting is so rich and chocolatey that it's hard to resist licking the spoon, and the finished cake is a showstopper, with its glossy frosting and tender crumb. It's the perfect dessert for anyone who loves chocolate, and it's sure to impress anyone who tries it.

Cake

2 tbsp (30 ml) melted butter, for the pan

2¼ cups (270 g) cake flour (page 191 or store-bought)

2¼ cups (450 g) granulated sugar

1¼ cups (112 g) Dutch process cocoa powder

2 tsp (9 g) baking powder

¼ tsp baking soda

1 tsp espresso powder

1 tsp salt

1½ cups (355 ml) hot water

1 cup (240 ml) olive, avocado or vegetable oil

4 large eggs, at room temperature

1 tbsp (15 ml) good-quality pure vanilla extract

Fudge Frosting

8 oz (226 g) 60% bittersweet chocolate (preferably Ghirardelli)

1½ cups (337 g) unsalted butter, softened

2 cups (240 g) confectioners' sugar

1 tsp espresso powder

1 tsp good-quality pure vanilla extract

⅛ tsp salt

2–3 tbsp (12–18 g) Dutch process cocoa powder (optional)

¼ cup (60 ml) heavy whipping cream

Prepare to bake. Preheat the oven to 350°F (175°C) with a rack in the middle. Line a 9 × 13–inch (23 × 33–cm) sheet pan with parchment paper and lightly brush it with melted butter using a silicone pastry brush. Leave some parchment paper hanging over the sides of the pan for easy removal of the cake. Set it aside.

Mix the ingredients. First, in a large bowl, whisk together the cake flour, sugar, cocoa powder, baking powder, baking soda, espresso powder and salt *(dry ingredients)* until combined. **Then,** gradually pour the hot water into the dry ingredients while stirring with a spatula. Set it aside to cool completely *(chocolate mixture)*. **Next,** whisk together the oil, eggs and vanilla in a separate medium bowl *(wet ingredients)*. **Finally,** once the chocolate mixture has cooled, pour the wet ingredients into it and beat with a hand mixer or whisk together until well combined.

Bake the cake. Scrape the batter into the prepared pan and bake for 25 to 35 minutes, or until a cake skewer or toothpick inserted into the center comes out clean. Once done, remove the cake from the oven and allow it cool in the pan for 10 minutes before transferring it to the cooling rack to cool completely.

Make the fudge frosting. First, melt the chocolate in a medium, microwave-safe bowl, heating it in the microwave at medium power (50%) for 60 to 90 seconds, stirring every 20 to 30 seconds, until fully melted. Set it aside to cool. **Next,** in a large bowl, use a hand mixer to beat the softened butter for 2 to 3 minutes, until light and creamy. Add the confectioners' sugar, espresso powder, vanilla, salt and cocoa powder. Beat until smooth. Stir in the cooled chocolate, beating until well incorporated. **Finally,** add the heavy whipping cream and beat for 1 minute, until everything is well mixed. Frost the cooled cake as desired.

South Indian Honey Cake

♣ Makes one 8-inch (20-cm) cake ♣

The South Indian honey cake is a popular and beloved baked good that originated from the Iyengar bakery, a chain of bakeries that started in Bangalore, India in the early 1900s. One of the most popular items on the Iyengar bakery's menu is the honey cake. They are eggless cakes, drenched with honey syrup, slathered with strawberry jam and sprinkled with desiccated coconut. Just describing the cake brings me so much nostalgia. For many people, the honey cake from Iyengar bakery is a delicious reminder of their childhood and a treasured part of their cultural heritage.

Cake

2 tbsp (30 ml) melted butter, for the pan

2 cups (250 g) all-purpose flour

1 cup (120 g) confectioners' sugar

1 tsp baking powder

½ tsp baking soda

½ tsp salt

1 tsp good-quality pure vanilla extract

½ cup (120 ml) vegetable oil

1 cup (240 ml) yogurt, at room temperature

½ cup (120 ml) condensed milk

½ cup (120 ml) fresh orange juice

Sugar Syrup

1 tbsp (13 g) granulated sugar

½ cup (120 ml) water

5 tbsp (75 ml) honey

½ tsp orange blossom water

For Assembly

3 tbsp (60 g) strawberry preserves

½ cup (35 g) unsweetened desiccated/shredded coconut or coconut powder (see Tip)

Prepare to bake. Preheat the oven to 350°F (175°C) with a rack in the middle. Line an 8 × 8–inch (20 × 20–cm) pan with parchment paper and lightly brush it with melted butter using a silicone pastry brush. Leave some parchment paper hanging over the sides of the pan for easy removal of the cake. Set it aside.

Mix the ingredients. First, in a large bowl, whisk together the flour, confectioners' sugar, baking powder, baking soda and salt *(dry ingredients)* until combined. **Next,** using a fork, whisk together the vanilla, oil, yogurt, condensed milk and orange juice in a separate medium bowl until all the ingredients are well combined *(wet ingredients)*. **Finally,** add the wet ingredients to the dry ingredients and whisk together gently until no streaks of flour are visible. It is okay to have small lumps. Avoid overmixing the batter.

Bake the cake. Spoon the batter into the prepared cake pan and bake for 35 to 45 minutes, or until a cake skewer or toothpick inserted into the center comes out clean. Allow the cake to rest in the pan for 5 to 10 minutes. Gently invert the cake onto the serving plate and peel off the parchment. Trim the sides of the cake and prick it all over.

Make the sugar syrup. Place sugar and water in a 4-cup (960-ml) microwave-safe measuring cup and heat in the microwave for 30 to 60 seconds, until the sugar dissolves. Set it aside to cool completely, then stir in the honey and orange blossom water.

Assembling the cake. Drizzle the syrup all over the cake, then spread the strawberry preserves on top and sprinkle the cake with desiccated coconut.

> ## Tip
> You can find unsweetened desiccated coconut or coconut powder in Indian/Asian grocery stores or on Amazon.

Badam Halwa Mini Cakes

♣ Makes seven 4-ounce (113-g) cakes ♣

Badam halwa is a decadent Indian dessert made with ground almonds, ghee and sugar. Known to be rich and infused with saffron, the pudding is a staple during special occasions and festivals in India. In this recipe, I've taken the flavors of badam halwa and turned them into mini cakes that are perfect for serving at a party or for individual treats. The richness of the almond pudding is encapsulated in this cake, and it's remarkably effortless to bake. It's crucial to use saffron and ghee for the ideal taste. Every bite of this cake will transport you to the splendid flavor of the dessert!

½ tsp saffron strands

¼ cup (60 ml) whole milk, hot

2 cups (208 g) almond flour

½ cup (64 g) all-purpose flour

1 tsp cardamom powder (page 188 or store-bought)

1 cup (200 g) granulated sugar

1 tsp baking powder

½ tsp salt

½ cup (104 g) ghee, melted and cooled (page 190 or store-bought)

2 large eggs, at room temperature

¾ cup (180 ml) whole milk, at room temperature

1 tbsp (7 g) sliced almonds

Tip

It's crucial to use saffron and ghee for the ideal taste, so do not use any substitutes or omit these ingredients.

Prepare to bake. Preheat the oven to 350°F (175°C) with a rack in the middle. Place seven 4-ounce (113-g) baking cups on a baking sheet.

Soak saffron in milk. In a small bowl, combine the saffron strands with the hot milk. Set it aside to cool completely *(saffron-milk mixture)*.

Mix the ingredients. First, in a large bowl, whisk together the almond flour, all-purpose flour, cardamom, sugar, baking powder, and salt *(dry ingredients)* until combined. **Then,** in a separate medium bowl, whisk together the cooled ghee, eggs and milk using a fork *(wet ingredients)*. **Now,** add the wet ingredients to the dry ingredients and mix gently with a whisk. **Finally,** fold in the saffron-milk mixture.

Bake the cakes. Divide the batter evenly among the seven baking cups. Sprinkle sliced almonds on top of each cake and bake for 25 to 35 minutes, or until a cake skewer or toothpick inserted into the center comes out clean. Remove the cakes from the oven and allow them to cool completely on the baking sheet.

Pumpkin-Chocolate Marble Loaf Cake

♣ Makes one 9 × 5–inch (23 × 13–cm) loaf cake ♣

Pumpkin and chocolate are a match made in heaven, and this marble loaf cake with maple glaze is the perfect example of that. This cake is perfect for fall and winter, with warm and cozy flavors that will make you want to curl up with a slice and a cup of hot cocoa. The pumpkin and chocolate batters are swirled together to create a beautiful marble effect, and the maple glaze adds just the right amount of sweetness. The cake is moist and fluffy, with just the right amount of pumpkin spice and chocolate flavor. Whether you're looking for a dessert to bring to a fall potluck or just want something delicious to enjoy at home, this loaf cake is sure to please. It's easy to make and even easier to enjoy, so don't hesitate to give it a try!

Pumpkin Batter

2 tbsp (30 ml) melted unsalted butter, for the pan

2 cups (240 g) cake flour (page 191 or store-bought)

2 tsp (9 g) baking powder

1 tsp baking soda

1 tsp salt

1 tsp pumpkin pie spice

1 cup (240 ml) olive, avocado or vegetable oil

2 cups (450 g) packed light brown sugar

4 large eggs, at room temperature

1 tbsp (15 ml) good-quality pure vanilla extract

¼ cup (60 ml) sour cream, at room temperature

1 cup (224 g) pumpkin puree

Chocolate Batter

2 cups (475 ml) pumpkin batter

1 tsp espresso powder

¼ cup (22 g) cocoa powder

Prepare to bake. Preheat the oven to 350°F (175°C) with a rack in the middle. Using a silicone pastry brush, grease a 9 × 5–inch (23 × 13–cm) loaf pan with melted butter. You can melt the butter for 20 to 30 seconds in the microwave. Line the bottom of the pan with parchment paper, making sure to leave some excess paper hanging over the sides for easy removal of the loaf.

Mix the dry ingredients. Add the cake flour, baking powder, baking soda, salt and pumpkin pie spice to a medium bowl. Whisk together until it's well combined *(dry ingredients)*.

Beat the fats and sugar and add all the wet ingredients. Using a hand mixer or a stand mixer fitted with a paddle attachment, beat the oil and brown sugar for 2 minutes. Scrape down the sides and the bottom of the bowl with a rubber spatula as needed. Add the eggs one at a time, beating well after each addition, scraping down the sides and the bottom of the bowl with a rubber spatula. Stir in the vanilla, sour cream and pumpkin puree. Beat until it's well mixed.

Add the dry ingredients. With the mixer on low speed, add all the dry ingredients and mix until just combined ensuring no streaks of flour remain *(pumpkin batter)*.

Prepare the chocolate batter. In a separate medium bowl, beat the pumpkin batter, along with the espresso powder and the cocoa powder. Set it aside *(chocolate batter)*.

(continued)

Pumpkin-Chocolate Marble Loaf Cake (continued)

Maple Glaze
¼ cup (60 ml) maple syrup

1 cup (120 g) confectioners' sugar

A pinch of salt

Bake the cake. To create a marbled effect, add a few spoonfuls of pumpkin batter to the bottom of the pan, then add a spoonful of chocolate batter on top. Repeat this process until all the batter is used, alternating between the two batters. Tap the loaf pan to remove any air bubbles and bake for 50 to 60 minutes. If the cake starts to brown too quickly, cover it with aluminum foil and continue baking for an additional 10 minutes. The cake is done when a cake skewer or toothpick inserted into the center comes out clean. Once done, remove the cake from the oven and let it cool in the pan for 10 minutes before transferring it to a cooling rack to cool completely.

Make the maple glaze. Whisk together the maple syrup, confectioners' sugar and salt in a medium bowl until smooth. Drizzle the glaze over the cooled cake.

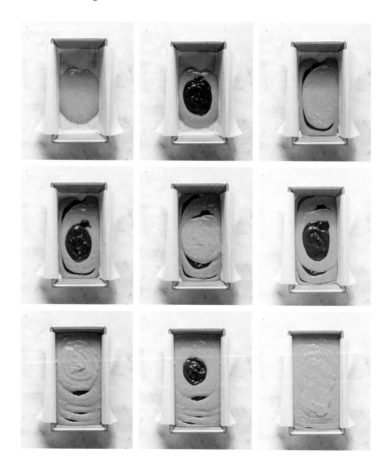

Sticky Toffee Pudding

♠ Makes 14 to 15 cupcakes ♠

Sticky toffee pudding with toffee sauce is a classic British dessert that is rich, sweet and absolutely indulgent. The cake is soft and moist, with a melt-in-your-mouth texture that comes from using mashed dates in the batter. The real star of the show, however, is the luscious toffee sauce that is poured over the warm cake. Made with butter, brown sugar, heavy cream and a touch of molasses, the sauce is rich and thick with a deep caramel flavor. It's the perfect topping for the warm cake and pairs beautifully with a scoop of vanilla ice cream.

Cake

2 cups (384 g) Medjool dates, chopped

1 cup (240 ml) boiling water

½ tsp baking soda

1¼ cups (150 g) cake flour (page 191 or store-bought)

1 tsp baking powder

¾ tsp salt

A pinch of nutmeg

¼ tsp ground cinnamon

½ tsp ground ginger

½ cup (112 g) unsalted butter, softened

½ cup (115 g) packed dark brown sugar

2 large eggs, at room temperature

3 tbsp (45 ml) vegetable oil

1 tsp good-quality pure vanilla extract

3 tbsp (60 g) molasses

Prepare to bake. Preheat the oven to 350°F (175°C) with a rack in the middle. Line a 12-cupcake tin with liners. Set it aside. **To soak the dates, place** the dates in a medium bowl. Pour the boiling water along with the baking soda into it. Set it aside.

Mix the dry ingredients. In a medium bowl, whisk together the cake flour, baking powder, salt, nutmeg, cinnamon and ginger *(dry ingredients)* until combined.

Beat the fats and sugar. In a large bowl, using a hand mixer or a stand mixer fitted with a paddle attachment, beat the butter and sugar for 3 to 4 minutes. Scrape down the sides and the bottom of the bowl with a rubber spatula as needed. Gradually beat in the eggs, one at a time, scraping down the sides and the bottom of the bowl with a rubber spatula. Stir in the oil, vanilla and molasses. Beat until just combined. Add the dry ingredients and beat until just combined, ensuring that no streaks of flour are visible.

Mash the dates. Using a fork or blender, mash or puree the soaked dates until they reach a smooth consistency (date puree).

Mix in the date puree to the cake batter. Incorporate the date puree into the cake batter and fold gently until well combined.

Bake the cake. Fill each cupcake tin two-thirds of the way with the batter. Bake for 20 to 25 minutes, or until a cake skewer or toothpick inserted into the center comes out clean.

(continued)

Sticky Toffee Pudding (continued)

Toffee Sauce

5 tbsp (70 g) butter, melted

1½ cups (340 g) packed dark brown sugar

1½ cups (355 ml) heavy whipping cream

1 tsp molasses

1 tsp good-quality pure vanilla extract

1 tsp rose salt

For Serving

Vanilla ice cream

Make the toffee sauce. While the cake is in the oven, prepare the toffee sauce. Add the butter to a 4-cup (960-ml) microwave-safe measuring cup and microwave for 30-second intervals, until the butter is fully melted. **Now,** add the brown sugar, heavy cream and molasses to the melted butter. Microwave the mixture for 3 minutes, stirring every 30 seconds. The toffee sauce will be bubbly and have a thin consistency after 3 minutes. Add the vanilla and the rose salt and give it a quick whisk. Set it aside to cool completely. The sauce will thicken as it cools down. Store any leftover sauce in an airtight container in the refrigerator for up to 2 weeks.

Assemble the sticky toffee pudding. After the cupcakes finish baking, let them rest in the pan for 5 to 10 minutes. Use a fork to gently prick the surface of the cake, then spoon some toffee sauce over each cupcake. Invert the cupcake onto a serving plate, remove the liner and add more sauce on top. Serve with a scoop of vanilla ice cream for the perfect finishing touch.

Baked Coconut Barfi

This baked coconut kalakand barfi recipe is a twist on the traditional coconut barfi that my mom used to make during Diwali. Instead of constantly stirring on the stovetop like with many Indian sweets, this baked version is easier and less intimidating. While it looks like a mini tea cake when it comes out of the oven, when you take a bite, you'll experience the chewy texture of a delicious barfi.

2 tbsp (25 g) shortening, for the pan

2 tbsp (16 g) all-purpose flour, for dusting the pan

½ cup (60 g) cake flour (page 191 or store-bought)

A pinch of salt

1½ cups (169 g) Baker's sweetened angel flake coconut

1 (14-oz [396-g]) can sweetened condensed milk

1 cup (250 g) whole-milk ricotta cheese, at room temperature lightly whisked with a fork

2 tbsp (26 g) ghee, at room temperature (page 190 or store-bought)

1 tbsp (15 ml) good-quality pure vanilla extract

Prepare to bake. Preheat the oven to 350°F (175°C) with a rack in the middle. Line a 12-count cupcake tin with liners or brush a mini tea cake pan with melted shortening, which can be melted in the microwave and used immediately without cooling. Use a silicone pastry brush to ensure all creases of the pan are covered, then dust the pan with flour.

Mix the ingredients. First, in a large bowl, whisk together the cake flour and salt *(dry ingredients)* until combined. **Next,** in a separate medium bowl, combine the sweetened coconut, condensed milk, ricotta cheese, ghee and vanilla. Whisk the mixture well until it is thoroughly combined *(wet ingredients)*. **Finally,** combine the dry ingredients with the wet ingredients and whisk together until the mixture is well combined and there are no visible streaks of flour.

Bake the barfi. Fill each tea cake or cupcake tin two-thirds of the way with batter and bake for 30 to 35 minutes, or until a cake skewer or toothpick inserted into the center comes out clean. Once the cake is baked, unmold the barfis immediately onto a cooling rack. If you're using a cupcake tin, you can skip this step.

Badam Paal Crème Brûlée

♠ Makes four 6-ounce (170-g) ramekins ♠

This crème brûlée is inspired by the flavors of badam paal, a saffron and almond milk drink from India that is enjoyed chilled in summers and piping hot in winters. Growing up in Chennai, my mom used to make chilled badam paal at home to help me and my sister combat the heat. I've melded the flavors of this delicious drink with the classic French dessert to create a custard with a subtle almond taste and a beautiful saffron flavor. To make this recipe more approachable for beginner bakers, I've used slow baking to avoid the water bath. This dessert is a fusion of French technique with the flavors of India, resulting in a delicious treat that is sure to impress anyone.

2 tbsp (18 g) whole almonds, blanched and skin removed

2 cups (475 ml) heavy whipping cream

¾ tsp saffron

2 tsp (4 g) cardamom powder (page 188 or store-bought)

4 egg yolks, at room temperature

½ cup (100 g) granulated sugar, plus more for topping

Prepare to bake. Preheat the oven to 200°F (93°C) with a rack in the middle. Place four 6-ounce (170-g) ramekins on a baking sheet.

Make the badam paal. Blend the almonds with ½ cup (120 ml) of cream to create a paste using a blender. After the paste has formed, add the remaining cream, saffron and cardamom. Blend until smooth. Transfer the mixture to a 4-cup (960-ml) microwave-safe measuring cup. Microwave the badam paal for 2 to 3 minutes, until it reaches a boil. Allow it to cool slightly until it becomes warm.

Whisk together the egg yolks and sugar. Whisk together the egg yolks and sugar in a separate large bowl until pale and well combined.

Temper the yolks with the warm badam paal. Slowly pour ¼ cup (60 ml) of the warm badam paal into the egg yolk mixture, whisking continuously to avoid cooking the yolks. Then, pour the egg mixture into the remaining badam paal and whisk thoroughly while pouring.

Bake the crème brûlée. Divide the mixture evenly among the ramekins and place them on the baking sheet on the middle rack of the oven. Cover the ramekins with aluminum foil lightly and bake at 200°F (93°C) for 1 hour, or until the centers are barely set. Allow the custards to cool completely, then refrigerate them until ready to serve.

Serve the crème brûlée. When ready to serve, sprinkle 1 table-spoon (13 g) of sugar evenly on top of each custard. Use a kitchen torch to melt the sugar and form a crispy top. If a kitchen torch is not available, turn on the oven broiler and place the ramekins in the oven for 2 minutes, or until the sugar is melted and nicely browned. Refrigerate the crème brûlée for at least 20 minutes before serving.

CRAVE-WORTHY
COOKIES & MADELEINES

From showstopping Jaggery Gingerbread Townhouse Cookies (page 69) to Kahlúa™-Glazed Ragi Chocolate Cookies (page 79) to Walnut Linzer Sables (page 71), this chapter offers a variety of beautiful holiday cookies that are sure to satisfy your sweet tooth. You will also find an array of Indian bakery cookies, such as Cardamom Ghee Biscuits (Nei Biscuit; page 75), Soan Papdi Cookies (page 76) and Kaju Pista Roll Pinwheels (page 81), with authentic flavors that will transport you to the streets of India. Each cookie in this chapter is a unique twist on a traditional cookie, making these treats perfect for any occasion.

In addition to mouthwatering cookies, this chapter also features the most delicious Orange Saffron Madeleines (page 63) and Red Velvet Madeleines (page 65). These are a beautiful addition to any dessert spread with their vibrant colors and irresistible taste. Whether you're a fan of classic cookies or crave a twist on traditional flavors, there is something here for everyone to enjoy.

Orange Saffron Madeleines

♣ Makes 12 to 14 madeleines ♣

These beauties are my twist on the classic French dessert. With the addition of saffron, these madeleines have a golden hue. The melted ghee adds a touch of *mithai* flavor, which is usually rich and decadent with a focus on sweetness balanced with subtle spices and aromatic flavors. The batter is left to rest in the refrigerator, allowing the flavors to meld and develop. Once baked, the madeleines develop the traditional hump on top, creating an iconic shape that is both beautiful and delicious. The rose water and honey syrup brushed over the top adds a burst of flavorful aroma. Sprinkled with pistachios, these madeleines are a perfect little treat to grace your Diwali table.

Madeleines

1 tbsp (15 ml) whole milk

½ tsp saffron

1¼ cups (150 g) cake flour (page 191 or store-bought)

½ tsp baking powder

1 tbsp (7 g) cardamom powder (page 188 or store-bought)

½ tsp salt

2 large eggs, at room temperature

2 egg yolks, at room temperature

¾ cup (150 g) granulated sugar

1 tsp orange blossom water

1 tsp orange zest

½ cup (104 g) ghee, melted and cooled (page 190 or store-bought)

2 tbsp (28 g) unsalted butter, for the pan

Prepare the saffron milk. Heat the milk in the microwave until hot, then remove it and add the saffron. Let the mixture sit to infuse and cool *(saffron milk)*.

Mix the ingredients. First, in a medium bowl, sift the cake flour, baking powder, cardamom and salt *(dry ingredients)*. **Next,** in a large clean bowl, beat the eggs, egg yolks and sugar. Start at a low speed for 1 minute and gradually increase the speed to high for 8 to 9 minutes, or until the mixture becomes light and fluffy and it has doubled in volume *(egg mixture)*. **Finally,** using a spatula, gently fold in the dry ingredients, orange blossom water, orange zest and saffron milk to the egg mixture. Take care not to deflate the eggs and keep folding until no streaks of flour are visible *(batter)*.

Prepare the batter, cover and place it in the fridge. Gently fold the cooled ghee into the batter. Cover the batter with plastic wrap, ensuring it touches the surface of the batter to prevent skin formation. Refrigerate the batter for at least 4 hours, overnight or up to 1 day.

At the same time, prepare the madeleine pan and place it in the freezer. Melt the butter and coat the madeleine pan using a pastry brush, making sure to cover all creases. Place the pan in the freezer for at least 15 to 20 minutes.

(continued)

Orange Saffron Madeleines (continued)

Rose Honey Syrup

½ tsp rose water

2 tbsp (30 ml) fresh orange juice

2 tbsp (30 ml) water

⅛ tsp saffron (optional)

⅛ tsp cardamom powder
(page 188 or store-bought)

¼ cup (60 ml) honey

2–3 tbsp (17–30 g) crushed raw
pistachios, for garnish

Preheat the oven and bake the madeleines. After chilling the batter, preheat the oven to 350°F (175°C). Remove the madeleine pan from the freezer and spoon 1½ to 2 tablespoons (25 to 30 ml) of batter into each mold and bake for 15 to 20 minutes, or until done. Be careful not to overbake (see Tip). Once done, invert the madeleines onto a cooling rack to cool completely.

Make the rose honey syrup. Combine the rose water, orange juice, water, saffron and cardamom in a small bowl. Warm it in the microwave for 30 seconds and set it aside to cool. Once cooled, add the honey and whisk together until well combined. Brush the mixture over the cooled madeleines and sprinkle some pistachios on top.

Tip

The madeleines should develop a traditional hump on top, but if they don't, they will still look and taste delicious.

Red Velvet Madeleines

♣ Makes 12 to 14 madeleines ♣

Whenever I bake these red velvet madeleines, my kids can't get enough of them. The light chocolate flavor combined with the cream cheese glaze makes for a delicious treat that's hard to resist. I prefer to use beet powder instead of artificial food coloring for a healthier twist. These madeleines are moist, fluffy and have just the right amount of cocoa to give them that classic red velvet flavor. The cream cheese glaze adds a tangy sweetness that complements the richness of the madeleines. Just be careful, not to overbake them; overbaking can lead to a dry texture and a hard madeleine. They are also beautifully shaped in heart molds, making them perfect for special occasions or to impress your loved ones. For those who prefer a subtler flavor, check out the variation at the end of the recipe.

Madeleines

1¼ cups (150 g) cake flour (page 191 or store-bought)

½ tsp baking powder

1 tbsp (5 g) cocoa powder

2–3 tbsp (14–27 g) beet powder or a few drops red food coloring (optional)

1 tsp salt

2 large eggs, at room temperature

2 egg yolks, at room temperature

¾ cup (150 g) granulated sugar

2 tsp (12 g) vanilla paste or 1 tbsp (15 ml) good-quality pure vanilla extract

1 tbsp (15 ml) olive oil

½ cup (112 g) unsalted butter, melted and cooled

2 tbsp (28 g) unsalted butter, for the pan

Sift all the dry ingredients. In a medium bowl, sift the cake flour, baking powder, cocoa powder, beet powder (if using) and salt (*dry ingredients*).

Beat the eggs, yolks and sugar. In a clean large bowl, beat the eggs, egg yolks and sugar. Start at a low speed for 1 minute and gradually increase the speed to high for 8 to 9 minutes, or until the mixture becomes light and fluffy and it has doubled in volume (*egg mixture*).

Mix the dry ingredients and flavorings into the egg mixture. Once the eggs are light and fluffy, gently fold in the dry ingredients, vanilla and oil using a spatula. Take care not to deflate the eggs and keep folding until no streaks of flour are visible (*batter*).

Prepare the batter, cover and place it in the fridge. Gently fold the cooled butter into the batter. Add the beet powder or red food coloring (if using) and gently mix until the color is all well mixed in the batter. Cover the batter with plastic wrap, ensuring it touches the surface of the batter to prevent skin formation. Refrigerate the batter for at least 4 hours, overnight or up to 1 day.

At the same time, prepare the madeleine pan and place it in the freezer. Melt the butter and coat the madeleine pan using a pastry brush, making sure to cover all creases. Place the pan in the freezer for 15 to 20 minutes.

(continued)

Cream Cheese Glaze

1½ cups (180 g) confectioners' sugar

3 tbsp (45 ml) whole milk

¼ tsp lemon extract or 1 tsp good-quality pure vanilla extract (optional)

3 oz (85 g) cream cheese, at room temperature

Preheat the oven and bake the madeleines. After chilling the batter, preheat the oven to 350°F (175°C). Remove the madeleine pan from the freezer and spoon 1 tablespoon (15 ml) of batter into each mold and bake for 8 to 10 minutes, or until a cake skewer or toothpick inserted into the center comes out clean. Be careful not to overbake. The madeleines should develop a traditional hump on top, but if they don't, they will still look and taste delicious. Once done, invert the madeleines onto a cooling rack to cool completely.

Make the cream cheese glaze. In a large bowl, mix the confectioners' sugar, milk and lemon extract (if using) until smooth. Then, add the cream cheese and mix well until the glaze is creamy and fully combined. Once the madeleines have cooled, dip them in the glaze and place them on a cooling rack to allow the glaze to set. Once completely cooled, store the madeleines in an airtight container for up to 2 days.

Variations

Brown Butter–Vanilla Madeleine: Use brown butter (page 189) instead of melted butter and omit the food coloring or beet powder and cocoa powder. You can also elevate the flavor by adding a vanilla bean, scraping the seeds and adding it to the batter. Just follow the instructions above and finish off by dusting the madeleines with confectioners' sugar when serving for a delicious, classic treat.

Jaggery Gingerbread Townhouse Cookies

♠ Makes 22 to 30 cookies ♠

These cookies are my take on a classic holiday treat. The combination of the spicy gingerbread flavor and the rich, caramel taste of jaggery creates a perfect balance of sweetness and warmth. Jaggery is a traditional sweetener commonly used in India and Southeast Asia. It is made from the sap of palm trees or sugarcane juice that is boiled to create a thick, dark caramel-like substance. It has a rich, distinctive flavor that often is described as earthy, nutty and smoky with notes of toffee and molasses. It is a perfect match for the warm spices and molasses in gingerbread, making these cookies a wonderful treat for the holidays.

Cookies

3½ cups (439 g) all-purpose flour

1 tbsp (6 g) ground ginger

¼ tsp ground cloves

1 tsp ground cinnamon

¼ tsp cardamom powder (page 188 or store-bought)

¼ tsp baking soda

¼ tsp salt

½ cup (112 g) unsalted butter, softened

1 cup (217 g) jaggery powder or dark brown sugar

1 large egg, at room temperature

2 tsp (10 ml) good-quality pure vanilla extract

½ cup (170 g) blackstrap molasses

1 tbsp (15 ml) water (optional)

1 tbsp (8 g) all-purpose flour (optional)

Sift the dry ingredients. In a medium bowl, sift the flour, ginger, cloves, cinnamon, cardamom, baking soda and salt *(dry ingredients)*.

Cream the fats and jaggery. With a hand mixer or a stand mixer fitted with a paddle attachment, cream the butter and jaggery for 2 to 3 minutes, until light and fluffy. Scrape down the sides and the bottom of the bowl with a rubber spatula as needed. Add the egg and beat until combined. Then, add the vanilla and blackstrap molasses. Beat until just mixed *(wet ingredients)*.

Combine the wet and the dry ingredients. With the mixer on low speed, add the dry ingredients to the wet mixture and mix until just combined. If the cookie dough is either too dry or too wet, simply add 1 tablespoon (15 ml) of water to the mixture if it is too dry or 1 tablespoon (8 g) of flour if it appears too wet. This will help bring the dough together and create the ideal consistency for rolling and cutting.

Wrap and chill the cookie dough. Divide the cookie dough into two equal halves and flatten them into circular discs with a diameter of about 4 to 5 inches (10 to 13 cm). Wrap each disc tightly in plastic wrap and place them in the refrigerator to chill for at least 2 hours or for up to 3 days.

(continued)

Jaggery Gingerbread Townhouse Cookies (continued)

Simple Icing

4 cups (480 g) confectioners' sugar

¾ cup (180 ml) heavy whipping cream

2 tsp (10 ml) imitation vanilla extract

Preheat the oven, roll and bake the cookies. Preheat the oven to 350°F (175°C). Line 2 to 3 baking sheets with parchment paper or silicone baking mats. Remove a disc of cookie dough from the refrigerator. Lightly flour the surface. Roll out to ¼-inch (6-mm) thickness between two sheets of parchment paper. Cut the dough into your desired townhouse cookie shapes. Don't worry if you don't have the townhouse cookie cutouts; you can easily use any cookie cutters you have on hand to create your desired shapes.

Use a dough scraper to carefully transfer the cut cookies onto the prepared baking sheets, placing them about 3 inches (7.5 cm) apart. Bake the cookies in the preheated oven for 8 to 12 minutes, or until the edges are lightly browned. Once they're done, take the baking sheets out of the oven and let the cookies cool on the baking sheet before transferring them to an airtight container. If you plan to frost the cookies, wait until they are cooled completely before doing so. Once completely cooled, store the cookies in an airtight container for up to 1 month.

Make the simple icing. In a medium bowl, combine the confectioners' sugar, heavy cream and vanilla. Using a hand mixer, beat until smooth. To adjust the consistency of the frosting, you can either add more cream (1 teaspoon at a time) if it's too thick, or more confectioners' sugar if it's too thin. Frost the cookies as desired.

Walnut Linzer Sables

♣ Makes 30 sandwich cookies ♣

Linzer cookies are a type of cookie with a nutty, buttery flavor that originates from the Austrian city of Linz. These cookies are a classic holiday favorite that I love to bake every year. The rich flavor of the walnuts is the perfect complement to the sweet, tangy strawberry jam filling. I've used cake flour in the recipe to give the cookies a delicate structure that simply melts in your mouth. With a light dusting of confectioners' sugar on top, they look as beautiful as they taste. These cookies are a wonderful addition to your holiday cookie tray, and they are sure to become a favorite with your family—just like they are for ours!

2¼ cups (270 g) cake flour (page 191 or store-bought)

1½ cups (180 g) walnut halves, ground with ¼ cup (30 g) cake flour (see Tip)

¼ tsp cardamom powder (page 188 or store-bought)

¼ tsp kosher salt

1 cup (225 g) unsalted butter, softened

1¼ cups plus 1 tbsp (158 g) confectioners' sugar, sifted

2 large egg yolks, at room temperature

1 tbsp (15 ml) heavy whipping cream

2 tsp (10 ml) good-quality pure vanilla extract

1 tsp orange or lemon zest

All-purpose flour, for rolling out the cookies

½ cup (160 g) strawberry jam

3 tbsp (24 g) confectioners' sugar, for dusting

Sift the dry ingredients. In a medium bowl, sift the cake flour, ground walnuts, cardamom and salt *(dry ingredients)*.

Cream the fats and sugar. Using a hand mixer or stand mixer fitted with a paddle attachment, beat the butter for 2 to 3 minutes, until it becomes light and fluffy. Scrape down the sides and the bottom of the bowl with a rubber spatula as needed. Add the sifted confectioners' sugar and beat until well combined. Add the egg yolks and beat until fully incorporated, scraping down the sides and the bottom of the bowl with a rubber spatula. Pour in the heavy whipping cream, vanilla and orange zest, and beat until just combined *(wet ingredients)*.

Combine the wet and the dry ingredients. With the mixer on low speed, add the dry ingredients to the wet mixture and mix until just combined.

Wrap and chill the cookie dough. Divide the cookie dough into two equal halves and flatten them into circular discs. Wrap each disc tightly in plastic wrap and place them in the refrigerator to chill for at least 2 hours or for up to 2 days.

(continued)

Walnut Linzer Sables (continued)

Tip

You can substitute ground walnuts with equal quantities of almond flour or hazelnut flour.

Preheat the oven, and roll and bake the cookies. Preheat the oven to 350°F (175°C). Line 2 to 3 baking sheets with parchment paper or silicone baking mats. Remove a disc of cookie dough from the refrigerator. Lightly flour the surface. Roll out the dough to ¼ inch (6 mm) thick between two sheets of parchment paper.

Use your favorite 2-inch (5-cm) Linzer cookie cutters to cut out the desired shapes, and carefully transfer the cut cookies onto the prepared baking sheets using a dough scraper. Make sure to leave at least 2 inches (5 cm) of space between each cookie. Bake the cookies for 8 to 9 minutes, or until the edges are lightly browned.

Remove the cookies from the oven and let them cool on the baking sheet for 5 minutes before transferring them to a cooling rack. Once completely cooled, store the cookies in an airtight container at room temperature for up to 1 week or freeze for up to 3 months.

Assemble the cookies. To fill the cooled cookies, spread a layer of jam on the bottom of one cookie and sprinkle confectioners' sugar on the bottom of another cookie. **Then,** sandwich the cookies together to form a Linzer cookie.

Cardamom Ghee Biscuits (Nei Biscuit)

♠ Makes 17 to 18 cookies ♠

This biscuit is an iconic snack in South India, and you can find them in every tea shop, usually stored in a glass jar. They are lightly sweetened and have a melt-in-your-mouth texture that makes them highly addictive. This biscuit is one of my all-time favorites to enjoy with afternoon tea. They bring back a flood of beautiful memories. The ghee gives them a rich and buttery flavor, and they are flavored with cardamom for a lovely aromatic touch. What's more, they are eggless, making them a perfect treat for lacto-vegetarians.

1¼ cups (150 g) cake flour (page 191 or store-bought)

⅛ tsp baking powder

1 tsp cardamom powder (page 188 or store-bought)

A pinch of salt

¾ cup (156 g) ghee, solid room temperature (page 190 or store-bought)

¾ cup plus 1 tbsp (98 g) confectioners' sugar, sifted

Sift the dry ingredients. In a medium bowl, mix together the cake flour, baking powder, cardamom and salt using a whisk *(dry ingredients)*.

Make the cookie dough. Add the ghee to a large bowl. Beat it using a hand mixer or stand mixer fitted with a paddle attachment for 2 to 3 minutes, until it's light and fluffy, scraping down the sides and the bottom of the bowl with a rubber spatula as needed. Sift the confectioners' sugar and mix it into the ghee on low speed. **Next,** add the dry ingredients and knead the dough by hand until it comes together. Wrap the dough in plastic wrap and refrigerate for 20 minutes to chill.

Preheat the oven and prepare the baking sheet. While the dough is chilling, preheat the oven to 350°F (175°C). Line 2 to 3 baking sheets with parchment paper or silicone baking mats.

Bake the cookies. Roll the chilled cookie dough into small (1-tablespoon [15-ml]) balls in the center of your palm. Flatten the balls with the impression of a fork and place them on the prepared baking sheet. Leave at least 2 inches (5 cm) of space between each cookie. Bake the cookies in the preheated oven for 12 to 13 minutes, or until the bottoms are lightly browned. Remove the baking sheets from the oven and let the cookies cool on the sheets for 10 minutes. It's important to let them cool before handling them, as they may break if you try to hold them right away. Once completely cooled, store the cookies in an airtight container or glass jar for up to 2 weeks.

Soan Papdi Cookies

♠ Makes 17 to 18 cookies ♠

These are my twist on the popular Indian sweet, *soan papdi*, made from sugar, gram flour and ghee. It is typically enjoyed during festive occasions, and it is known for its light and flaky texture. By using the same ingredients in a different form, I transformed this traditional Indian sweet into a melt-in-your-mouth treat that's sure to satisfy your sweet tooth. This recipe eliminates the daunting process of making soan papdi, making it easy for anyone to enjoy the delectable taste in the form of a cookie.

2 cups (240 g) besan flour or chickpea flour

2 cups plus 1 tbsp (248 g) confectioners' sugar, sifted

¾ cup (156 g) ghee, melted and cooled (page 190 or store-bought)

2 tbsp (17 g) crushed raw pistachios, for garnish

Prepare to bake and toast the besan flour. Preheat the oven to 350°F (175°C). Spread the besan flour on a baking sheet and bake it for about 7 minutes. Once done, remove the baking sheet from the oven and let the flour cool completely before using it in the recipe. While the flour cools, line a second baking sheet with parchment paper or a silicone baking mat.

Make the cookie dough. In a large bowl, sift the toasted besan flour and confectioners' sugar (dry ingredients). Drizzle the ghee over the dry ingredients and use your hands to knead the dough gently until it just comes together.

Bake the cookies. Using a 1-tablespoon (15-ml) cookie scoop, drop the cookies onto the prepared baking sheet, spacing them about 2 inches (5 cm) apart. Bake the cookies in the preheated oven for 14 to 18 minutes, or until the bottoms are lightly browned. Remove the baking sheet from the oven and let the cookies cool on the baking sheet for at least 2 hours. It's important to let them cool and dry out completely before handling them, as they may crumble or stick if you try to hold them right away. Sprinkle some pistachios on top of each cookie for garnish. Once completely cooled, store the cookies in an airtight container for up to 1 week.

Kahlúa™-Glazed Ragi Chocolate Cookies

These are a delightful twist on the classic chocolate chip cookie, perfect for the holiday season. The *ragi flour*, also known as finger millet flour, adds a lovely nuttiness and earthiness to the cookies, while the Kahlúa-glaze adds a rich and boozy touch. I have used a stamped rolling pin to create a beautiful vintage tile pattern on the cookies, making them a stunning addition to any cookie platter.

Cookies

1 cup (125 g) ragi/finger millet flour

2 cups (250 g) all-purpose flour, plus more for rolling out cookies

½ cup (45 g) Dutch process cocoa powder

1 tsp espresso powder

½ tsp salt

1 cup (225 g) unsalted butter, softened

½ cup (115 g) packed dark brown sugar

½ cup (100 g) granulated sugar

1 large egg, at room temperature

1 large egg yolk, at room temperature

2 tsp (10 ml) good-quality pure vanilla extract

Toast the ragi flour in the oven. Preheat the oven to 350°F (175°C), spread the ragi flour on a baking sheet, and bake it for about 5 minutes. Once done, remove the baking sheet from the oven and let the flour cool completely before using it in the recipe.

Mix the ingredients. First, in a medium bowl, sift the all-purpose flour, ragi flour, cocoa powder, espresso powder and salt *(dry ingredients)*. **Next,** using a hand mixer or stand mixer fitted with a paddle attachment, beat the butter, brown sugar and granulated sugar for 2 to 3 minutes, until it becomes light and fluffy, scraping down the sides and the bottom of the bowl with a rubber spatula as needed. Add the egg, egg yolk and vanilla and beat until fully incorporated *(wet ingredients)*. **Finally,** with the mixer on low speed, add the dry ingredients to the wet ingredients and mix until just combined.

Wrap and chill the cookie dough. Divide the cookie dough into two equal halves and flatten them into circular discs. Wrap each disc tightly in plastic wrap and place them in the refrigerator to chill for at least 2 hours or for up to 2 days.

Preheat the oven, roll and bake the cookies. Preheat the oven to 350°F (175°C). Line 2 to 3 baking sheets with parchment paper or silicone baking mats. Remove a disc of cookie dough from the refrigerator and lightly flour the surface. Roll out the dough to ¼-inch (6-mm) thickness between two sheets of parchment paper. **Next,** using the stamped rolling pin, firmly roll over the dough to make a pattern all over the surface. **Then,** use cookie cutters to cut the dough into desired shapes. Use a dough scraper to carefully transfer the cut cookies onto the prepared baking sheets, making sure to leave at least 2 inches (5 cm) of space between each cookie. Bake the cookies in the preheated oven for 7 to 8 minutes, or until the edges are lightly browned.

(continued)

Kahlúa™-Glazed Ragi Chocolate Cookies (continued)

Kahlúa Icing

1 cup (120 g) confectioners' sugar

¼ cup (60 ml) heavy cream

1 tsp Kahlúa liquor or coffee extract

1 tsp vanilla extract

Make the glaze. While the cookies are baking, whisk together the confectioners' sugar, heavy cream, Kahlúa liquor and vanilla in a small bowl.

Glaze the cookies. Once the cookies are finished baking, remove them from the oven and immediately brush the hot cookies with the glaze using a silicone pastry brush. The cookies will take on a beautiful vintage tile appearance as the glaze dries up. Let the cookies cool on the baking sheet for 10 to 15 minutes before transferring them to a cooling rack to cool completely. Once completely cooled, store the cookies in an airtight container for up to 3 days.

Kaju Pista Roll Pinwheels

I was inspired to create these *kaju pista* pinwheel cookies after seeing how much my husband enjoyed the traditional Indian sweet, kaju pista roll. Using the same combination of cashews and pistachios, I transformed the flavors into an eggless cookie with a soft and buttery texture. The pinwheel design not only adds a beautiful touch to the cookies but also creates a perfect snack for teatime or any occasion. These cookies are sure to be a hit with anyone who loves nutty, delicious treats!

Kaju Cookies

1 cup (120 g) cake flour (page 191 or store-bought)

1 cup (137 g) raw cashews, ground with 1 tbsp (8 g) cake flour

1 tsp cardamom powder (page 188 or store-bought)

¼ tsp salt

12 tbsp (168 g) unsalted butter, softened

1 cup plus 1 tbsp (128 g) confectioners' sugar, sifted

Pista Cookies

1 cup (120 g) cake flour (page 191 or store-bought)

1 cup (123 g) unsalted raw pistachios, ground with 1 tbsp (8 g) cake flour

¼ tsp salt

12 tbsp (168 g) unsalted butter, softened

1 cup plus 1 tbsp (128 g) confectioners' sugar, sifted

1 tsp rose water

Mix the kaju cookie dough. First, in a medium bowl, mix together the cake flour, ground cashews, cardamom and salt using a whisk *(dry ingredients)*. **Next,** using a hand mixer or stand mixer fitted with a paddle attachment, beat the butter for 2 to 3 minutes, until it becomes light and fluffy, scraping down the sides and the bottom of the bowl with a rubber spatula as needed. Add the sifted confectioners' sugar and beat until well combined *(wet mixture)*. **Finally,** with the mixer on low speed add the dry ingredients to the wet mixture and mix until just combined.

Wrap and chill the kaju cookie dough. After preparing the cookie dough, shape it into a disc and wrap it tightly in plastic wrap. **Then,** place it in the refrigerator and let it chill for at least 2 hours or up to 2 days.

Mix the pista cookie dough ingredients. First, in a medium bowl, mix together the cake flour, ground pistachios and salt using a whisk *(dry ingredients)*. **Next,** using a hand mixer or stand mixer fitted with a paddle attachment, beat the butter for 2 to 3 minutes, until it becomes light and fluffy, scraping down the sides and the bottom of the bowl with a rubber spatula as needed. Add the sifted confectioners' sugar and beat until well combined. Stir in the rose water *(wet ingredients)*. **Finally,** with the mixer on low speed add the dry ingredients to the wet mixture and mix until just combined.

Wrap and chill the pista cookie dough. After preparing the cookie dough, shape it into a disc and wrap it tightly in plastic wrap. **Then,** place it in the refrigerator and let it chill for at least 2 hours or up to 2 days.

(continued)

Kaju Pista Roll Pinwheels (continued)

All-purpose flour, for rolling out the cookies

Roll and shape the cookie dough. Start by rolling out a large rectangle of kaju dough between two sheets of parchment paper. Repeat this process with the pista dough and lightly sprinkle flour on the dough to prevent it from sticking. Peel off the top sheet of the parchment paper from each dough and flip the pista dough over onto the kaju dough. Trim any excess dough to create a perfect rectangle and gently run a rolling pin over the dough to ensure that the two layers stick together. If the dough is sticky, sprinkle a bit more flour on top. **Next,** tightly roll the dough into a log and use a sharp knife to cut the log in half. Wrap each half in plastic wrap. To avoid wasting any excess trimmings, gently roll them into small logs and wrap them in plastic wrap as well. Refrigerate these logs for at least 3 hours or freeze them for 30 minutes.

Preheat the oven, slice and bake the cookies. Preheat the oven to 350°F (175°C). Line 2 to 3 baking sheets with parchment paper or silicone baking mats. Using a sharp knife, slice the dough into ¼-inch (6-mm)-thick rounds and place them on the prepared baking sheets, leaving 3 inches (7.5 cm) of space between each cookie. Bake the cookies for 11 to 14 minutes, until the kaju dough is slightly golden. The small logs can be baked for about 7 minutes, until lightly browned. Let the cookies cool completely on the baking sheet until they are fully set, then transfer the cookies onto a cooling rack. Once completely cooled, store the cookies in an airtight container for up to 1 week.

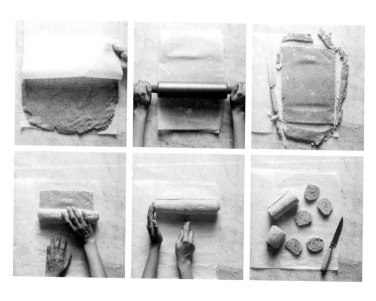

Rose Cookies (Achu Murukku)

Achu murukku is an Indian snack that is very similar to the popular Scandinavian rosette cookies. Made with rice flour, coconut milk, eggs and vanilla, these delicate, crispy cookies are a nostalgic treat for many who grew up with them. I have fond memories of my grandmom making these for us every year during Christmas. As a kid, I couldn't get enough of these addictive cookies, and even now they are the only deep-fried snack I can't seem to control myself around. The cookies are very lightly sweetened and have a crunchy texture that makes them a perfect teatime snack. Achu murukku is a traditional Christmas treat in many Indian households, and they are often made in large batches and shared with friends and family.

1½ cups (237 g) white rice flour

2 tbsp (16 g) all-purpose flour

¾ cup (90 g) confectioners' sugar, sifted

¼ tsp salt

2 large eggs, at room temperature

1 (13-oz [403-ml]) can unsweetened coconut milk

1 cup (240 ml) water

1½ tbsp (25 ml) vanilla extract

8 cups (1.9 L) vegetable oil, for frying

Prepare the rosette mold. If you're using a nonstick mold, it can be used as is without any preparation. If you are using an iron or aluminum mold, it's essential to treat it before use: Wash the mold thoroughly, then heat some oil and soak the mold for at least 2 days.

Mix the ingredients. First, in a large bowl, whisk together the rice flour, all-purpose flour, sifted confectioners' sugar and salt *(dry ingredients)*. **Next,** in a medium bowl, beat the eggs, coconut milk, water and vanilla using a whisk *(wet ingredients)*. **Finally,** combine the wet and dry ingredients, and whisk together until the mixture forms a thin and smooth batter with a consistency similar to that of crepe batter.

Make the cookies. Heat the oil in a large, wide, heavy-bottomed pan to 350°F (175°C). Dip the mold in the oil for at least 15 seconds to heat it up. **Next,** dip the heated mold into the thin batter so that three-quarters of the mold is immersed in the batter. The batter should stick to the mold. Carefully dip the mold into the preheated oil, making sure to dip the mold in the oil each time before dipping in the batter. Leave the mold in the oil for a few seconds, then shake the mold for the murukku to release. When the murukku starts to get slightly brown on one side, gently flip it onto the other side and fry until it is golden brown on both sides. Only fry 2 murukkus maximum at a time and bring the oil back to the correct temperature between batches. You'll will know it is done cooking when the oil stops sizzling and calms down. Remove the murukkus and drain them on a paper towel. Once completely cooled, store the achu murukku in an airtight container for up to 2 weeks.

CELEBRATORY
CAKES & FANCY DESSERTS

This chapter is a true feast for the eyes and the taste buds! It features a wide range of layer cakes including Funfetti Cake with Rice Krispies® Filling (page 89) and Cardamom-Pecan-Pumpkin Layer Cake (page 91). For those looking for Indian-inspired flavors, there's the Green Nut Cake (page 133), Christmas Rum Fruitcake (page 121), Strawberry Lassi–Coconut Layer Cake (page 111) and Malai Sandwich Layer Cake (page 103). And who can resist a classic German Chocolate Layer Cake (page 115) or Boston Cream Pie (page 117)?

But the selection doesn't stop at cakes. You'll also find indulgent desserts such as Kahlúa™ Tiramisu Cake (page 95), Flourless Chocolate Torte with Mocha Mousse (page 101) and Hazelnut Vanilla Torte (page 107), as well as some fancy desserts made effortlessly simple, including the Easy Pavlova (page 123), Cream Puffs (page 127) and French Canelés (page 129).

Whether you're celebrating a special occasion or simply want to treat yourself, this chapter has got you covered. Each recipe is carefully crafted to ensure a perfect balance of flavors and textures, leaving you wanting more. From the bold and exotic to the classic and refined, there's no shortage of options to satisfy any craving. So, go ahead and indulge in a slice of one of these celebratory cakes or fancy desserts—you deserve it!

Funfetti Cake with Rice Krispies® Filling

♠ Makes one 8-inch (20-cm) three-layer cake ♠

Looking for a fun birthday cake that will be a hit with both kids and adults? Look no further than this funfetti cake with Rice Krispies filling, frosted with a rich cream cheese icing. The cake itself is a moist white cake batter, studded with colorful sprinkles for a festive touch. The true standout element of this cake is the Rice Krispies filling, providing a delightful crunch and unique twist to a traditional birthday cake. The icing gives a tangy balance to the sweet flavors of the cake.

White Cake

3½ cups (420 g) cake flour (page 191 or store-bought)

1 tbsp (14 g) baking powder

1 tsp salt

¾ cup (168 g) unsalted butter, softened

2 cups (400 g) granulated sugar

1 cup (240 ml) grapeseed or vegetable oil

1 tbsp (15 ml) clear imitation vanilla extract or pure vanilla extract

½ tsp almond extract

¾ cup (180 ml) sour cream, at room temperature

1 cup (240 ml) whole milk, at room temperature

6 large egg whites, at room temperature

¾ cup (144 g) rainbow jimmies

Prepare to bake. Preheat the oven to 350°F (175°C) with a rack in the middle. Spray three 8-inch (20-cm) pans with nonstick cooking spray. Line the bottoms of the pans with parchment paper.

Mix the ingredients. First, in a medium bowl, whisk together the cake flour, baking powder and salt *(dry ingredients)*. **Then,** in a large bowl using a hand mixer or a stand mixer with a paddle attachment, beat the butter for 2 to 3 minutes, until it is pale, light and fluffy, scraping down the sides and the bottom of the bowl with a rubber spatula as needed. **Next,** add the sugar and oil and beat for 2 to 3 minutes, until well combined. Scrape down the sides and the bottom of the bowl with a rubber spatula. Mix in the vanilla and almond extracts until just combined *(butter-sugar mixture)*. **Finally,** incorporate the dry ingredients into the butter-sugar mixture in three batches, alternating with the addition of the sour cream and milk. Begin and end with the dry ingredients. Set the batter aside *(cake batter)*.

Beat the egg whites to stiff peaks and fold in the batter. In a large, clean bowl, using a hand mixer or stand mixer with the whisk attachment, beat the egg whites on low speed for 1 minute and increase to high speed for 3 to 5 minutes, until stiff peaks form. Gradually and gently fold the whipped egg whites in batches of three into the cake batter. **Finally,** fold the rainbow jimmies into the batter.

Bake the cake. Evenly divide the batter among the prepared cake pans. Give the pans a gentle tap to remove any air bubbles and bake for 20 to 30 minutes, or until a cake skewer or toothpick comes out clean. Once finished, remove the cakes from the oven and let them sit in the pan for 1 minute before gently inverting them onto cooling racks. Allow the cakes to cool completely before filling and frosting. If you plan to frost later, you can wrap the cakes in plastic wrap and place them in the refrigerator or freezer.

(continued)

Funfetti Cake with Rice Krispies® Filling (continued)

Rice Krispies Cereal Filling

2½ cups (420 g) white chocolate chips

3 cups (80 g) Rice Krispies cereal

Cream Cheese Frosting

2 (8-oz [226-g] each) boxes cream cheese, at room temperature

1 cup (225 g) unsalted butter, softened

1 cup (240 ml) heavy whipping cream, cold

3–4 cups (360–480 g) confectioners' sugar

1 tbsp (15 ml) clear imitation vanilla extract or pure vanilla extract

1 tsp salt

Simple Syrup Soak

2 tbsp (26 g) granulated sugar

¼ cup (60 ml) water

Variation

For a variation on this funfetti cake, you can swap the Rice Krispies filling with ¾ cup (240 g) of raspberry preserves for a beautiful white raspberry layer cake. Simply omit the rainbow jimmies from the cake batter and follow the same baking instructions. You'll still have a rich and moist white cake with a creamy cream cheese frosting with a fruity twist from the raspberry filling.

Make the Rice Krispies filling. While the cakes cool, start making the filling. In a large, microwave-safe bowl, melt the white chocolate chips in the microwave at medium power (50%) for 30 to 60 seconds, stirring every 20 to 30 seconds, until fully melted. Let the white chocolate mixture cool. In a large bowl, mix the Rice Krispies cereal with the melted white chocolate and fold until well combined. Spread the mixture evenly on a lined baking sheet and place it in the freezer for about 5 minutes. Then, crumble the filling and set it aside.

Make the frosting. Using a hand mixer or a stand mixer fitted with a paddle or whisk attachment, beat the cream cheese and butter in a large bowl until it's smooth and creamy, scraping down the sides and the bottom of the bowl with a rubber spatula. Then, gradually add the heavy whipping cream and continue beating. Next, add 3 cups (360 g) of confectioners' sugar, along with the vanilla and salt. Beat on low speed for 30 seconds before switching to high speed and beating for 2 minutes. If you prefer sweeter frosting, feel free to add an extra ½ to 1 cup (60 to 120 g) of confectioners' sugar.

Make the simple syrup soak. In a small, microwave-safe glass bowl, microwave the sugar and water for 30 to 60 seconds, until the sugar has melted. Set it aside *(simple syrup)*.

Assemble the layer cake. First, level the cakes with a serrated knife if needed. To achieve the same appearance as the cake shown in the picture, you can utilize an 8-inch (20-cm) cake ring to cut the cake edges and expose the sprinkles. **Next,** place a small amount of frosting on the bottom of an 8-inch (20-cm) cake board and place the first cake layer on top. Brush the simple syrup onto the cake's surface with a pastry brush. **Then,** spread a generous amount of frosting evenly with an offset spatula, then pipe a border around the edges to keep the filling in place. Add one-third of the filling inside the border before adding the next cake layer on top. Repeat with the remaining cake layers and filling. Apply a thin layer of frosting all over the cake using the offset spatula. For a firmer frosting, chill the cake in the refrigerator briefly. Decorate the cake as desired and store the cake in the refrigerator until serving. Let the cake sit out at room temperature for at least 1 hour before serving.

Cardamom-Pecan-Pumpkin Layer Cake

♠ Makes one 8-inch (20-cm) three-layer cake ♠

This cake is the perfect treat for fall! With a moist pumpkin cake, sweet and salty pecans, and a caramel cream cheese frosting, every bite is bursting with the warm and cozy flavors of the season. The layers of cake are filled with a decadent caramel sauce that perfectly complements the spice of the cardamom and the nuttiness of the pecans. The caramel cream cheese frosting adds a touch of tanginess to balance out the sweetness. Generously filled with pecans and caramel sauce, this cake is a stunning display of beauty and flavor.

Salted Caramel Sauce

1 cup (225 g) packed dark brown sugar

3 tbsp (42 g) unsalted butter, softened

½ cup plus 2 tbsp (150 ml) heavy cream, at room temperature

1 tsp good-quality pure vanilla extract

½ tsp rose salt

Sweet and Salty Pecans

1 tbsp (14 g) unsalted butter, softened

2 cups (224 g) pecan halves

5 tbsp (75 ml) maple syrup

½ tsp fine salt

1 tsp good-quality pure vanilla extract

Cardamom Pumpkin Cake

3 cups (360 g) cake flour (page 191 or store-bought)

2 tsp (9 g) baking powder

1 tsp baking soda

1 tsp pumpkin spice powder

2 tsp (4 g) cardamom powder (page 188 or store-bought)

1 tsp salt

1¼ cups (250 g) granulated sugar

½ cup (115 g) packed light brown sugar

4 large eggs, at room temperature

Make the salted caramel sauce. Combine the brown sugar, butter and heavy cream in a large measuring cup. Microwave the mixture for 3 minutes, stirring every 30 seconds. Keep an eye on the mixture as it will bubble up as it cooks. Once it turns golden caramel in color, it is ready. Immediately add the vanilla and salt and whisk together until smooth and uniform in color. Refrigerate until needed, then reheat in the microwave for 30 seconds at a time, stirring after each cycle until the sauce is fluid again. This caramel sauce can be stored in the refrigerator for 1 to 2 weeks.

Make the sweet and salty pecans. Preheat the oven to 300°F (150°C) with a rack in the middle. Line a baking sheet with parchment paper. In a medium saucepan over low to medium heat, melt the butter. Add the pecans and stir for 1 minute. **Then,** add the maple syrup, salt and vanilla and continue stirring for 2 to 3 minutes, until the pecans absorb the syrup. Switch off the heat. **Next,** spread the pecans on the prepared baking sheet, making sure to separate each pecan to prevent sticking once they're baked. Bake for 5 to 6 minutes, remove them from the oven and allow them to cool in the baking sheet until they're dry. **Finally,** store the pecans in an airtight container at room temperature.

Prepare to bake the cake. Increase the oven temperature to 350°F (175°C). Spray three 8-inch (20-cm) pans with nonstick cooking spray and line the bottoms of the pans with parchment paper.

Mix the ingredients. First, in a medium bowl, whisk together the cake flour, baking powder, baking soda, pumpkin spice powder, cardamom and salt *(dry ingredients)*. **Next,** using a hand mixer, beat the granulated sugar, brown sugar and eggs for 4 to 5 minutes, until they become light and fluffy, scraping down the bowl as needed.

(continued)

Cardamom-Pecan-Pumpkin Layer Cake (continued)

1 cup (240 ml) olive, avocado or vegetable oil

1¾ cups (427 g) canned pumpkin puree

1 tbsp (15 ml) good-quality pure vanilla extract

½ cup (120 ml) sour cream, at room temperature

Caramel Cream Cheese Frosting

8 oz (226 g) cream cheese, at room temperature

1½ cups (337 g) unsalted butter, softened

½ cup (120 g) caramel sauce (see Tip)

1–1½ cups (120–180 g) confectioners' sugar, plus more to taste

½ tsp salt

Tip

You can also use store-bought caramel sauce. You will need about 1 to 1½ cups (240 ml to 360 ml) of caramel sauce for filling and frosting.

Next, add the oil, pumpkin puree, vanilla and sour cream and beat until well combined *(wet ingredients)*. **Finally,** add the dry ingredients to the wet ingredients and mix on low speed until just combined.

Bake the cake. Evenly divide the batter among the prepared cake pans. Give the pans a gentle tap to remove any air bubbles and bake for 20 to 30 minutes, or until a cake skewer or toothpick comes out clean. Once finished, remove the cakes from the oven and let them sit in the pan for 1 minute before gently inverting them onto cooling racks. Allow the cakes to cool completely before filling and frosting. If you plan to frost later, you can wrap the cakes in plastic wrap and place them in the refrigerator or freezer.

Make the frosting. Using a hand mixer or a stand mixer fitted with a paddle or whisk attachment, beat the cream cheese and butter in a large bowl until it's smooth and creamy, scraping down the sides and the bottom of the bowl with a rubber spatula as needed. Then, gradually add the thick caramel sauce and continue beating. **Next,** add 1 to 1½ cups of confectioners' sugar to taste and the salt. Beat on low speed for 30 seconds before switching to high speed and beating for 2 minutes. If you prefer a sweeter frosting, feel free to add an extra ½ to 1 cup (60 to 120 g) of confectioners' sugar.

Assemble the layer cake. Remove the domes from your cakes using a serrated knife, if needed. For easy assembly, consider freezing your cakes in plastic wrap for 30 minutes. Alternatively, spread a small amount of frosting on the bottom of an 8-inch (20-cm) cake board and place the first layer on top. Apply a generous amount of frosting on the first layer, spreading it evenly with an offset spatula, then pipe a border around the edges to keep the filling in place. Spoon ¼ cup (60 ml) of caramel sauce and arrange ½ to ¾ cup (56 to 84 g) of sweet and salty pecans on top inside the border, before adding the next layer of cake. Repeat this process with the remaining layers of cake. Use the offset spatula to apply a thin layer of frosting all over the cake, giving it a rustic, "naked" look. Chill the cake in the refrigerator for 15 minutes, then decorate as desired and serve at room temperature. Leftovers can be stored in an airtight container in the refrigerator for up to 4 days. Let the cake sit out at room temperature for at least 1 hour before serving.

Kahlúa™ Tiramisu Cake

♠ Makes one 9-inch (23-cm) two-layer cake ♠

As someone who adores coffee desserts, this cake is one of my absolute favorites. This cake features a light, airy genoise cake soaked in a rich coffee mixture, then frosted with a velvety mascarpone frosting. The result is a cake that's incredibly moist and packed with flavor. As you prepare this cake, be sure to follow all the tips carefully to ensure that the frosting comes out perfectly. The mascarpone frosting is a delicate mixture that requires gentle handling, so it's important to use cold mascarpone cheese and heavy whipping cream straight from the refrigerator. Be sure to beat the frosting on low speed and avoid overbeating, as this can cause the cheese to curdle. With its irresistible combination of coffee and mascarpone, this cake is sure to become one of your favorites as well. Enjoy a slice with your morning coffee or serve it as the perfect dessert for any occasion.

Genoise Cake

1½ cups (180 g) cake flour (page 191 or store-bought)

2 tsp (9 g) baking powder

1 tsp salt

¾ cup (180 ml) whole milk, at room temperature

½ cup (120 ml) olive, avocado or vegetable oil

4 large eggs, at room temperature

2 large egg yolks, at room temperature

1½ cups (300 g) granulated sugar

1 tbsp (15 ml) good-quality pure vanilla extract

¼ tsp almond extract

Prepare to bake. Preheat the oven to 350°F (175°C) with a rack in the middle. Spray two 9-inch (23-cm) pans with nonstick cooking spray and line the bottoms of the pans with parchment paper.

Mix the ingredients. First, in a medium bowl, whisk together the cake flour, baking powder and salt *(dry ingredients)*. **Now,** whisk together the milk and oil in a spouted measuring cup using a fork *(milk mixture)*. Set it aside. **Then,** using a hand mixer or a stand mixer with a paddle attachment, beat the eggs, egg yolks, sugar, vanilla and almond extract on medium speed for 5 minutes. Increase the speed to high and continue beating for 10 minutes, or until the mixture has tripled in volume *(wet ingredients)*. **Finally,** combine the dry ingredients and wet ingredients in a mixing bowl, then mix on low speed until they are just combined. Be careful not to overmix the batter. Once everything is incorporated, use a spatula to fold in the milk mixture until fully combined.

Bake the cake. Divide the batter equally between the prepared cake pans. Tap the pans gently to remove any air bubbles and bake for 20 to 30 minutes, or until a cake skewer or toothpick inserted into the center of the cake comes out clean. Once done, remove the cakes from the oven and let them cool in the pan for 1 minute before inverting them onto cooling racks. Allow the cakes to cool completely before frosting. If you plan to frost later, wrap the cakes in plastic wrap and store in the refrigerator or freezer. It is recommended to make the frosting on the day you plan to frost the cake.

(continued)

Kahlúa™ Tiramisu Cake (continued)

Mascarpone Frosting

2 cups (480 g) mascarpone cheese, cold straight from the refrigerator

1¾–2 cups (210–240 g) confectioners' sugar

2 tsp (10 ml) Kahlúa liquor

1½ cups (355 ml) heavy whipping cream, cold

Kahlúa Coffee Soak

¼ cup (60 ml) hot coffee

2 tbsp (26 g) granulated sugar

3 tbsp (45 ml) Kahlúa liquor

Tip

To avoid curdling, it's important to use cold mascarpone cheese straight from the refrigerator since heavy whipping cream is also cold. Avoid overbeating and beating the frosting on high speed.

Make the frosting. Using a hand mixer or stand mixer fitted with a paddle or whisk attachment, beat the cold mascarpone cheese, confectioners' sugar and Kahlúa liquor on low speed for 1 minute, until it is just combined, scraping down the sides and the bottom of the bowl with a rubber spatula as needed. **Then,** gradually add the cold heavy whipping cream and continue to beat on low speed for about 6 minutes, or until stiff peaks form. It's important to use cold cheese and cream. Avoid overbeating the frosting or beating it on high speed, as the cheese may curdle and ruin the entire frosting.

Make the Kahlúa soak. Combine the hot coffee, sugar and Kahlúa liquor in a small bowl. Whisk together to combine.

Assemble the layer cake. Trim any domes off your cakes using a serrated knife, if needed. You can also freeze the cakes briefly in plastic wrap for 10 to 15 minutes for easier handling. Alternatively, spread a small amount of frosting on the bottom of a 9-inch (23-cm) cake board and place the first cake layer on top. Using a pastry brush, apply the Kahlúa soak onto the surface of the cake. **Next,** apply a generous amount of frosting to the first layer and spread it evenly with an offset spatula. Repeat this process with the remaining cake layers. Use the offset spatula to apply a thin layer of frosting all over the cake, creating a rustic, "naked" look. Chill the cake in the refrigerator for 30 to 60 minutes, then decorate it as desired. Leftovers can be stored in an airtight container for up to 3 days.

Mango Cloud Cake

♠ Makes three 8-inch (20-cm) layer cakes ♠

Here we have a soft chiffon cake layered with mango mousse and juicy chunks of mango, enrobed in whipped cream. The cake is incredibly light and airy, similar to a light sponge cake but fluffier. The refreshing mousse and fresh mangoes provide the perfect complement to the cake's delicate flavor. The beautiful combination of flavors and textures in this cake is sure to leave you craving for more.

Sponge Cake

2 cups (240 g) cake flour (page 191 or store-bought)

2 tsp (9 g) baking powder

¼ tsp salt

6 large egg yolks, at room temperature

1½ cups (300 g) granulated sugar, divided

½ cup (120 ml) whole milk, at room temperature

⅔ cup (160 ml) olive, avocado or vegetable oil

1 tbsp (15 ml) good-quality pure vanilla extract

6 large egg whites, at room temperature

½ tsp cream of tartar

Prepare to bake. First, chill a mixing bowl and whisk/beaters in the refrigerator for the frosting. It's important to keep the mixing bowl very cold to achieve the desired consistency. **At the same time,** preheat the oven to 350°F (175°C) with a rack in the middle. Spray three 8-inch (20-cm) cake pans with nonstick cooking spray and line the bottoms of the pans with parchment paper.

Mix the ingredients. First, in a medium bowl, sift the cake flour, baking powder and salt *(dry ingredients)*. **Next,** in a separate medium bowl, whisk the egg yolks until they are pale and well mixed. Add 1 cup (200 g) of sugar to the egg yolks and mix well. **Then,** pour in the milk, oil and vanilla and whisk the mixture until it's smooth. Gently fold in the sifted dry ingredients and set the batter aside *(batter)*.

Beat the egg whites to stiff peaks and fold in the batter. To start, prepare a large, clean bowl. **Then,** using a hand mixer or a stand mixer with a whisk attachment, whisk together the egg whites and cream of tartar on low speed for 1 to 2 minutes, until frothy. Add the remaining ½ cup (100 g) of sugar and beat on high for 7 to 8 minutes, until stiff peaks form. Gently and gradually fold the whipped egg whites into the cake batter in batches of three.

Bake the cake. Divide the batter equally between the prepared cake pans. Tap the pans gently to remove any air bubbles and bake for 20 to 25 minutes, or until a cake skewer or toothpick inserted into the center of the cake comes out clean. Once done, remove the cakes from the oven and let them cool in the pan. Allow the cakes to cool completely before frosting. If you plan to frost later, wrap the cakes in plastic wrap with the pan and store them in the refrigerator. It is best to make the mango mousse filling and the frosting on the same day when you plan to frost the cake.

(continued)

Mango Cloud Cake (continued)

Mango Mousse Filling

1 tsp unflavored gelatin

4 tsp (20 ml) water

1 cup (240 ml) heavy whipping cream, cold

½ cup (60 g) confectioners' sugar

1 cup (175 g) chopped mango, pureed

Whipped Cream Frosting

1 tsp unflavored gelatin

4 tsp (20 ml) water

1¾ cups (410 ml) heavy whipping cream, cold

1½ cups (180 g) confectioners' sugar

1 tsp good-quality pure vanilla extract

¼ tsp salt

Simple Syrup Soak

2 tbsp (26 g) granulated sugar

¼ cup (60 ml) water

For Layering

2 cups (350 g) chopped mango

Make the mango mousse filling. First, bloom the gelatin in the water in a small, microwave-safe bowl. Set it aside for 5 minutes, then melt it in the microwave for about 5 seconds. Be cautious not to overheat it as it may curdle the cream. Cool to room temperature. **Next,** in the chilled mixing bowl, using the chilled beaters, beat the heavy whipping cream and confectioners' sugar on medium speed until soft peaks form. **Then,** drizzle in the melted gelatin mixture while still mixing on low speed. Keep mixing until the peaks become firm enough to hold their shape, but be sure not to overmix. **Finally,** gradually fold in the mango puree with the stabilized whipped cream. Set it aside.

Make the whipped cream frosting. First, bloom the gelatin in the water in a small microwave-safe bowl. Set it aside for 5 minutes, then melt it in the microwave for about 5 seconds. Be careful not to overheat it or it may curdle the cream. Cool to room temperature. In a chilled mixing bowl using hand mixers, beat the heavy whipping cream, confectioners' sugar, vanilla and salt on medium speed until soft peaks form. **Then,** drizzle in the melted gelatin mixture while continuing to mix on low speed. Keep mixing until the peaks are firm enough to hold their shape, but be sure not to overmix.

Make the simple syrup soak. In a small, microwave-safe glass bowl, microwave the sugar and water for about 30 to 60 seconds, until the sugar has melted. Set it aside.

Assemble the layer cake. Prepare an 8-inch (20-cm) cake board by spreading a small amount of frosting on the bottom. Place the first cake layer on top, and lightly brush the surface with the simple syrup soak using a pastry brush. Spread a generous amount of mango mousse on top of the first layer with an offset spatula and add an even layer of mangoes. Repeat this process with the remaining cake layers. Apply a thin layer of whipped cream frosting as a crumb coat and chill the cake in the fridge for 10 to 15 minutes. Once chilled, apply a final layer of whipped cream and use a bench scraper to smooth it out. Decorate with the remaining whipped cream and mango chunks to your liking. Leftovers can be stored in the refrigerator in an airtight container for up to 2 days.

Flourless Chocolate Torte with Mocha Mousse

♠ Makes one 9-inch (23-cm) cake ♠

This decadent dessert features a fudgy chocolate torte made with olive oil, creating a flavorful twist. The layers of smooth and creamy mocha mousse add a touch of coffee flavor that perfectly complements the rich, chocolatey goodness of the torte. The use of olive oil instead of butter makes the torte incredibly moist and easy to make. The mocha chocolate mousse layers are perfectly balanced with the fresh raspberries, adding a burst of fruity flavor to this luxurious dessert. So go ahead and treat yourself to this indulgent dessert that is sure to satisfy any chocolate craving.

Flourless Chocolate Torte

16 oz (454 g) 60% bittersweet chocolate (preferably Ghirardelli)

1 cup (240 ml) olive oil

8 large eggs, at room temperature

1 cup (200 g) granulated sugar

½ tsp espresso powder

1 tbsp (15 ml) good-quality pure vanilla extract

¼ tsp kosher salt

Prepare to bake. First, chill a mixing bowl and whisk/beaters in the refrigerator for the frosting. It's important to keep the mixing bowl very cold to achieve the desired consistency. **At the same time,** preheat the oven to 350°F (175°C) with a rack in the middle. Spray a 9-inch (23-cm) springform pan, at least 3 inches (7.5 cm) in height, with nonstick cooking spray. Line the bottom of the pan with a round parchment paper and the sides with long strips.

Melt the chocolate. In a large, microwave-safe bowl, add the chocolate and heat it in the microwave oven at medium power (50%) for 60 to 90 seconds. Make sure to stir every 20 to 30 seconds, until the chocolate has fully melted. Set it aside to cool completely *(melted and cooled chocolate).*

Mix the ingredients and bake the torte. First, whisk the oil into the cooled chocolate until combined, followed by one egg at a time until all the eggs are well incorporated. **Next,** add the sugar, espresso powder, vanilla and salt and gently whisk together until everything is fully mixed. Scrape the batter into the prepared cake pan and bake for 25 to 35 minutes, or until a cake skewer or toothpick inserted into the center of the cake comes out clean. Remove the cake from the oven and let it cool in the pan while you make the mocha mousse.

(continued)

Mocha Mousse Filling

1 tsp unflavored gelatin

4 tsp (20 ml) water

8 oz (226 g) semisweet chocolate (preferably Ghirardelli)

1½ cups (355 ml) heavy whipping cream, cold, divided

1 tsp espresso powder or Kahlúa liquor

1½ cups (190 g) fresh raspberries

Whipped Cream

1 tsp unflavored gelatin

4 tsp (20 ml) water

1½ cups (355 ml) heavy whipping cream, cold

¼ cup (30 g) confectioners' sugar

1 tsp good-quality pure vanilla extract

For Serving (optional)

1 tbsp (5 g) cocoa powder

Make the mocha mousse filling. First, bloom the gelatin in the water in a small bowl. Set it aside for 5 minutes to soften. **Next,** in a large, microwave-safe bowl, combine the chocolate and ½ cup (120 ml) of heavy whipping cream. Heat the mixture in the microwave at medium power (50%) for 60 to 90 seconds, stirring every 20 to 30 seconds, until the chocolate is fully melted. Remove the bowl from the microwave and add the softened gelatin. Stir until the gelatin is fully dissolved and the mixture is smooth. Add the espresso powder and give it a quick mix. Set it aside to cool completely *(chocolate-gelatin mixture)*.

Then, in the chilled mixing bowl, using the chilled beaters, beat the remaining 1 cup (240 ml) of heavy cream on medium speed for 1 minute, gradually increasing the speed to high and beat for 4 to 6 minutes, until stiff peaks form. Gradually fold in the stabilized whipped cream to the chocolate-gelatin mixture in two batches until no streaks appear. Gently fold in the fresh raspberries. **Finally,** spread the mousse evenly over the top of the cooled torte layer and refrigerate while you make the whipped cream.

Make the whipped cream. First, bloom the gelatin in the water in a small microwave-safe bowl. Set it aside for 5 minutes, then melt it in the microwave for about 5 seconds. Be cautious not to overheat it as it may curdle the cream. Cool to room temperature. **Next,** in a chilled mixing bowl using chilled hand mixers, beat the heavy whipping cream, confectioners' sugar and vanilla on medium speed until soft peaks form. **Then,** drizzle in the melted gelatin mixture while continuing to mix on low speed. Keep mixing until the peaks are firm enough to hold their shape, but be sure not to overmix. Spread or pipe the cream evenly over the mousse layer and refrigerate the cake for at least 2 hours and up to 24 hours. If refrigerating overnight, lightly cover the cake with plastic wrap.

Serve the torte. For the cleanest slices, dip a knife in warm water before cutting. To finish, dust the cake with cocoa powder (if using). Leftovers can be stored in an airtight container in the refrigerator for up to 3 days.

Malai Sandwich Layer Cake

♠ Makes three 8-inch (20-cm) layer cakes ♠

This is a twist on the traditional Indian dessert *chum chum* sweet, transformed into a stunning layer cake. Chum chum is a popular dish that is made by soaking oblong-shaped cottage cheese dumplings in a sugar syrup. The dumplings are filled with a mixture of khova and nuts, then rolled in desiccated coconut, and a sweetened cherry is placed in the center to give them a distinctive texture and flavor. Here, I have incorporated the delicious flavors of this sweet and created a layered cake version. The moist, fluffy ricotta cake layers are brushed with a fragrant saffron syrup, then stacked with a luscious saffron crème mousse and a crunchy khoya nut crumble. Then the cake is topped with desiccated coconut and garnished with sweet cherries.

Khova (Mawa)

½ cup (34 g) nonfat dry milk powder

½ tsp ghee (page 190 or store-bought)

¼ cup plus 2 tbsp (90 ml) heavy whipping cream

Khova (Mawa) Nut Filling

3 tbsp (42 g) unsalted butter

¾ cup (90 g) cake flour (page 191 or store-bought)

½ tsp baking powder

½ cup (64 g) mixed nuts, such as cashews, almonds and pistachios, chopped

¼ tsp cardamom powder (page 188 or store-bought)

3 tbsp (45 g) packed light brown sugar

Prepare to bake. Chill a large mixing bowl and whisk/beaters in the refrigerator for the frosting. It's important to keep the mixing bowl very cold to achieve the desired consistency. Preheat the oven to 300°F (150°C) with a rack in the middle. Line a baking sheet with parchment paper.

Make the khova. To prepare the khova, combine the milk powder, ghee and heavy whipping cream in a large, microwave-safe bowl. Microwave on high in 30-second intervals for 2 to 3 minutes, stirring every 30 seconds, until the mixture has dried up and formed a solid mass. Once the khova is ready, allow it to cool completely before using.

Make the khova nut filling. First, melt the butter in a small, microwave-safe bowl for about 30 seconds, until fully melted. Set it aside to cool completely. **Next,** in a mixing bowl, combine the cake flour, baking powder, khova, nuts, cardamom and sugar. Use a hand mixer to beat the mixture until well combined. **Then,** add the melted butter and beat on low speed for 30 seconds, or until small clusters begin to form. Spread the clusters on the prepared baking sheet and bake for 20 minutes. Once done, remove the pan from the oven and let the clusters cool completely before using.

(continued)

Malai Sandwich Layer Cake (continued)

Ricotta Cake

3 cups (360 g) cake flour (page 191 or store-bought)

1 tbsp (14 g) baking powder

½ tsp baking soda

1 tbsp (7 g) cardamom powder (page 188 or store-bought)

1 tsp salt

1¾ cups (350 g) granulated sugar

3 large eggs, at room temperature

1 cup (240 ml) grapeseed oil or any neutral oil

½ tsp saffron warmed in 1 tbsp (15 ml) milk

1 cup (250 g) ricotta cheese, at room temperature

¾ cup (180 ml) buttermilk, at room temperature

Saffron Malai Cream Mousse

1 tsp unflavored gelatin

4 tsp (20 ml) water

½ cup (120 ml) condensed milk, at room temperature

1½ cups (355 ml) heavy whipping cream, cold

1 cup (120 g) confectioners' sugar

½ tsp saffron, soaked in 1 tsp warm milk

Increase the oven temperature and mix the ingredients. Increase the oven temperature to 350°F (175°C). Spray three 8-inch (20-cm) pans with nonstick cooking spray and line the bottoms of the pans with parchment paper. In a medium bowl, whisk together the cake flour, baking powder, baking soda, cardamom and salt *(dry ingredients)*. **Next,** in a separate large bowl, using a hand mixer or a stand mixer with a paddle attachment, beat the sugar and eggs until they become light and fluffy for 4 to 5 minutes, scraping down the sides and the bottom of the bowl with a rubber spatula as needed. **Next,** add the oil, saffron and ricotta cheese. Beat until it is well combined *(wet ingredients)*.

Combine the wet and the dry ingredients and bake the cake. Add half the dry ingredients to the wet ingredients with the mixer on low speed, mixing until well combined. **Then,** stir in the buttermilk and add the remaining dry ingredients. Mix on low speed until just combined. Evenly divide the batter among the prepared cake pans. Give the pans a gentle tap to remove any air bubbles, then place them on the middle rack of the oven. Bake for 20 to 30 minutes, or until a cake skewer or toothpick comes out clean. Once finished, remove the cakes from the oven and let them sit in the pan for 1 minute before gently inverting them onto cooling racks. Allow the cakes to cool completely before filling and frosting. If you plan to frost later, you can wrap the cakes in plastic wrap and place them in the refrigerator or freezer.

Make the saffron malai cream mousse filling. First, bloom the gelatin in the water in a small, microwave-safe bowl. Set it aside for 5 minutes. Then melt it in the microwave for about 5 seconds. Be cautious not to overheat it as it may curdle the cream. **Then,** in the chilled mixing bowl, using the chilled beaters, beat the condensed milk, heavy cream, confectioners' sugar and saffron on medium speed for 1 minute. Continue to beat on medium-high speed until soft peaks form, which should take about 4 to 5 minutes. **Finally,** drizzle in the melted gelatin mixture while continuing to mix on low speed. Be sure not to overmix, but keep mixing until the peaks become firm enough to hold their shape. Store the mousse filling in the refrigerator until you are ready to frost.

(continued)

Malai Sandwich Layer Cake (continued)

Saffron Syrup Soak

2 tbsp (26 g) granulated sugar

¼ cup (60 ml) water

A pinch of saffron

For Topping

½ cup (35 g) unsweetened desiccated coconut/coconut powder

½ cup (70 g) maraschino cherries

Make the saffron syrup. In a small, microwave-safe glass bowl, microwave the sugar, water and saffron for 30 to 60 seconds, until the sugar has melted. Set it aside *(saffron simple syrup)*.

Assemble the layer cake. Prepare an 8-inch (20-cm) cake board by spreading a small amount of frosting on the bottom. Place the first cake layer on top, brush the saffron simple syrup onto the cake's surface with a pastry brush, and then generously spread the saffron malai cream mousse with an offset spatula, adding an even layer of khova nut filling. Repeat this process with the remaining cake layers. Use the offset spatula to fill in any gaps with the mousse, then use a bench scraper to slightly scrape off the edges for a rustic, "naked" look. Chill the cake in the refrigerator for about 1 hour.

Add the cake toppings. Sprinkle desiccated coconut over the cake and garnish with maraschino cherries. Leftovers can be stored in the refrigerator in an airtight container for up to 2 days.

Hazelnut Vanilla Torte

♠ Makes two 9 × 13–inch (23 × 33–cm) sheet cakes ♠

This torte, also known as Esterházy torte, is a delectable dessert comprised of hazelnut layers brushed with apricot syrup and layered with custard buttercream. A glaze is poured over the top, and it is finished with a feathered chocolate topping. At first glance, it may seem complicated due to its numerous components, but it is actually quite easy to make as the pastry cream is entirely made in the microwave. The time put into this cake is definitely worth it, as it results in a stunning and scrumptious dessert that is sure to impress.

Pastry Cream

1 cup (240 ml) whole milk

½ cup (120 ml) half-and-half

6 large egg yolks, at room temperature

½ cup (100 g) granulated sugar

¼ cup (32 g) cornstarch

1 vanilla bean, split lengthwise, seeds scraped

Hazelnut Sponge Cake

1½ cups (210 g) hazelnut flour

½ cup (60 g) cake flour (page 191 or store-bought)

¼ tsp kosher salt

6 large egg whites, at room temperature

¼ tsp cream of tartar

1 cup (200 g) granulated sugar

1 tbsp (15 ml) good-quality pure vanilla extract

Make the pastry cream. In a 2-quart (1.9-L) glass measuring bowl, whisk together the milk, half-and-half, egg yolks, sugar and cornstarch, using a whisk until the mixture is smooth. Then, microwave the mixture on high, in 30-second intervals for 5 to 7 minutes, stirring every 30 seconds, until the pastry cream has a thick and glossy custard-like consistency. Strain the mixture into a medium bowl, add the scraped vanilla seeds and, using a whisk, combine until smooth. Cover the bowl with plastic wrap, making sure the wrap touches the surface of the pastry cream and refrigerate until ready to use.

Prepare to bake. Preheat the oven to 350°F (175°C) with a rack in the middle. Spray two 9 × 13 × 0.75–inch (23 × 33 × 1.5–cm) sheet pans with nonstick cooking spray and line the bottoms of the pans with parchment paper.

Sift the dry ingredients. In a medium bowl, sift the hazelnut flour, cake flour and salt *(dry ingredients)*.

Beat the egg whites to stiff peaks and fold in the dry ingredients. In a clean bowl, using a hand mixer or a stand mixer with a whisk attachment, whisk together the egg whites and cream of tartar on low speed for 1 to 2 minutes, until frothy. Add the sugar and beat on high for 7 to 8 minutes, until stiff peaks form. Stir in the vanilla. Gently and gradually fold the dry ingredients into the whipped egg whites in two batches.

(continued)

Hazelnut Vanilla Torte (continued)

Custard Buttercream Frosting
4 sticks (454 g) unsalted butter, softened

½ cup plus 2 tbsp (76 g) confectioners' sugar

Simple Apricot Syrup Soak
¼ cup (60 ml) water

½ cup (160 g) apricot jam

Glaze
2 cups (240 g) confectioners' sugar

2 tbsp (30 ml) whole milk

½ tsp good-quality pure vanilla extract

Bake the cake. Evenly pour the batter into the prepared cake pans. Give the pans a gentle tap to remove any air bubbles and bake for 20 to 22 minutes, or until a cake skewer or toothpick inserted into the center of the cake comes out clean. Remove the pans from the oven and use a sharp knife to run along the edges of the pan to loosen the cake. Carefully invert each cake onto a sheet of parchment paper, peel off the parchment paper while the cake is still warm and allow it to cool completely.

Make the custard buttercream frosting. Using a hand mixer or a stand mixer fitted with a paddle attachment, beat the softened butter in a large mixing bowl for about 4 to 5 minutes, until light and creamy, scraping down the sides and the bottom of the bowl with a rubber spatula as needed. Add the confectioners' sugar and beat for 2 minutes. Whisk the chilled pastry cream until it reaches a smooth, custard-like consistency. Reduce the mixer speed to low and gradually pour the custard into the butter mixture in 3 to 4 additions, waiting until each addition is fully incorporated before adding the next. Set it aside.

Make the simple apricot syrup soak. In a small, microwave-safe glass bowl, heat up the water until it is very hot, then stir in the apricot jam and whisk it well. Set it aside *(simple apricot syrup)*.

Prepare the glaze and melt the chocolate for assembly. First, whisk together the confectioners' sugar, milk and vanilla to prepare the glaze. Set it aside. **Next,** add the chocolate to a medium, microwave-safe bowl. Heat it in the microwave oven at medium power (50%) for 20 to 30 seconds, stirring the chocolate every 10 seconds, until it has fully melted. Once melted, whisk the chocolate until smooth. Transfer the melted chocolate to a piping bag, and snip a very small opening at the bottom.

(continued)

Hazelnut Vanilla Torte (continued)

For Assembly

2 oz (57 g) semisweet chocolate

½ cup (56 g) sliced almonds

Assemble the layer cake. First, cut four equal-sized rectangles from the two sheet cakes and set aside the excess pieces. The thin rectangles that remain can be combined to form the fifth piece. **Next,** spread a small amount of the custard buttercream on the bottom of a rectangular cake board and place the first cake layer on top. Brush the surface of the cake with simple syrup using a pastry brush, then spread a generous amount of frosting, about ¾ cup (180 ml), on the first layer with an offset spatula and spread it evenly. Repeat this process with the remaining cake layers. **Then,** use an offset spatula to apply a layer of frosting all over the cake, and use a bench scraper to create a perfectly shaped rectangle by lightly scraping the sides of the cake. Gently pour the glaze over the top layer of the cake. Pipe 4 to 5 thin lines of chocolate along the length of the cake, and use a toothpick to create a feathered effect by drawing lines in the opposite direction of the chocolate. **Finally,** enrobe the sides of the cake with sliced almonds. Keep the cake chilled until you serve. Leftovers can be stored in an airtight container in the refrigerator for up to 2 days.

Strawberry Lassi–Coconut Layer Cake

♠ Makes three 8-inch (20-cm) layer cakes ♠

This cake is a refreshing twist on a classic *lassi*, a traditional yogurt-based drink that originated on the Indian subcontinent. It is a refreshing beverage that is made by blending yogurt, water and various seasonings and flavorings. This light and fluffy cake, infused with the refreshing taste of strawberry lassi, combined with the subtle hints of cardamom and rose water, is the perfect dessert for a hot summer day. The whipped cream and cream cheese frosting is the perfect complement to the cake, and the addition of shredded coconut adds a delightful texture. It is wonderful on any occasion, from birthdays to summer gatherings.

Strawberry Lassi

1 cup (145 g) fresh strawberries, hulled and chopped

¼ cup (50 g) granulated sugar

½ cup (120 ml) plain Greek yogurt, at room temperature

½ cup (120 ml) whole milk, at room temperature

¼ tsp cardamom powder (page 188 or store-bought)

2 tsp (10 ml) rose water or rose milk syrup

Cake

3 cups (360 g) cake flour (page 191 or store-bought)

2½ tsp (11 g) baking powder

½ tsp baking soda

1 tsp salt

1 cup (225 g) unsalted butter, softened

1½ cups (300 g) granulated sugar

3 large eggs, at room temperature

1 tbsp (15 ml) good-quality pure vanilla extract

½ cup (120 ml) grapeseed or vegetable oil

Few drops of red food coloring

Prepare to bake. Preheat the oven to 350°F (175°C) with a rack in the middle. Spray three 8-inch (20-cm) pans with nonstick cooking spray and line the bottoms of the pans with parchment paper.

Make the strawberry lassi in the blender. Add the strawberries and sugar to a blender and blend until smooth. Add in the yogurt, milk, cardamom and rose water and continue blending until everything is well combined and the mixture is smooth *(strawberry lassi)*.

Mix the ingredients. First, in a medium bowl, whisk together the cake flour, baking powder, baking soda and salt *(dry ingredients)*. **Next,** in a large bowl, use a hand mixer or a stand mixer with a paddle attachment to beat the butter until it turns pale, light and fluffy for 2 to 3 minutes. **Then,** add the sugar and beat for 2 to 3 minutes, until they are well combined. Add one egg at a time, making sure to beat well after each addition until all the eggs have been incorporated. Throughout this process, you may scrape down the sides and the bottom of the bowl with a rubber spatula as needed. Mix in the vanilla and oil and continue to beat until everything is combined *(wet ingredients)*. **Finally,** incorporate the dry ingredients into the wet ingredients in two batches, alternating with the strawberry lassi. Be sure to begin and end with the dry ingredients. Then add the food coloring and mix gently. Set the batter aside *(cake batter)*.

(continued)

Strawberry Lassi–Coconut Layer Cake (continued)

Whipped Cream Cheese Frosting

2 (8-oz [226-g] each) boxes cream cheese, at room temperature

1 cup (240 ml) heavy whipping cream, cold

½ cup (120 ml) sweetened condensed milk

1 cup (120 g) confectioners' sugar

1 tbsp (15 ml) good-quality pure vanilla extract

A generous pinch of salt

For Assembly

1–1½ cups (113–169 g) Baker's sweetened angel flake coconut, for enrobing

Bake the cake. Evenly divide the batter among the prepared cake pans. Give the pans a gentle tap to remove any air bubbles, then place them on the middle rack of the oven. Bake for 20 to 30 minutes, or until a cake skewer or toothpick comes out clean. Once finished, remove the cakes from the oven and let them sit in the pan for 1 minute before gently inverting them onto cooling racks. Allow the cakes to cool completely before filling and frosting. If you plan to frost later, you can wrap the cakes in plastic wrap and place them in the refrigerator or freezer.

Make the frosting. Using a hand mixer or a stand mixer fitted with a paddle or whisk attachment, beat the cream cheese and heavy whipping cream in a large bowl for about 30 to 60 seconds. Then, gradually add the sweetened condensed milk and confectioners' sugar and continue beating at medium speed for 2 to 3 minutes. Add the vanilla and salt. Beat on low speed for 10 seconds, until just mixed.

Assemble the layer cake. Make sure the cakes are leveled with a serrated knife if necessary. You can either briefly freeze the cakes wrapped in plastic or apply a small amount of frosting to the bottom of an 8-inch (20-cm) cake board and place the first cake layer on top. Apply a generous amount of frosting to the first layer and spread it evenly with an offset spatula, repeating this process with the remaining cake layers. Use the offset spatula to apply a thin layer of frosting all over the cake, and for a firmer frosting, chill the cake in the refrigerator for 30 to 60 minutes. Decorate the cake to your liking and cover the entire cake with coconut flakes. Store the cake in the refrigerator until ready to serve. Leftovers can be stored in an airtight container in the refrigerator for up to 3 days.

German Chocolate Layer Cake

♠ Makes three 8-inch (20-cm) layer cakes ♠

German chocolate cake is a classic dessert that is loved by many. The origins of the cake can be traced back to the mid-nineteenth century when a man named Samuel German created a new type of dark baking chocolate for the Baker's Chocolate company. The chocolate was named after him and soon became a popular ingredient in recipes, including this cake. This moist, rich chocolate cake is layered with a coconut pecan frosting that adds a perfect balance of sweetness and nuttiness. What makes my spin on this cake extra special is that the frosting is prepared completely in the microwave, making it easier and less intimidating to make.

Cake

4 oz (113 g) good-quality semisweet chocolate, chopped (preferably Ghirardelli)

½ cup (113 g) unsalted butter, at room temperature

2 cups (250 g) all-purpose flour

2 cups (400 g) granulated sugar

½ cup (45 g) Dutch process cocoa powder

1 tsp espresso powder

¾ tsp kosher salt

2 tsp (9 g) baking powder

¼ tsp baking soda

2 large eggs, at room temperature

1 tbsp (15 ml) good-quality pure vanilla extract

½ cup (120 ml) sour cream or plain Greek yogurt, at room temperature

½ cup (120 ml) olive, avocado, vegetable or canola oil

1 cup (240 ml) hot water

Prepare to bake. Preheat the oven to 350°F (175°C) with a rack in the middle. Spray three 8-inch (20-cm) pans with nonstick cooking spray and line the bottoms of the pans with parchment paper.

Melt the chocolate and add the butter. In a large, microwave-safe bowl, add the chocolate and heat it in the microwave oven at medium power (50%) for 60 to 90 seconds. Make sure to stir every 20 to 30 seconds, until the chocolate has fully melted. **Next,** add the stick of softened butter. Mix well using a spatula until the butter is fully melted and combined with the chocolate. Set the mixture aside to cool *(chocolate mixture).*

Mix the ingredients. First, in a medium bowl, whisk together the flour, sugar, cocoa powder, espresso powder, salt, baking powder and baking soda *(dry ingredients).* **Then,** in a small bowl or a glass measuring cup, combine the eggs, vanilla, sour cream and oil. Beat the mixture using a fork and set it aside *(wet ingredients).* **Then,** using a whisk, add the dry ingredients to the chocolate mixture and mix well. **Now,** add the wet ingredients to the batter, and combine until all the ingredients are well mixed and no streaks of flour are visible. **Finally,** pour the hot water into the batter and mix until the batter looks smooth.

(continued)

German Chocolate Layer Cake (continued)

German Chocolate Frosting

2 cups (220 g) roughly chopped pecans

1 cup (240 ml) evaporated milk

1 cup (220 g) packed light or dark brown sugar

4 large egg yolks, at room temperature

½ tsp salt

½ cup (112 g) unsalted butter, melted and cooled

1 tbsp (15 ml) good-quality pure vanilla extract

2 cups (226 g) Baker's sweetened angel flake coconut

Tip

You can drizzle ganache over the cake. To make the ganache, in a microwave-safe glass measuring cup, heat ¾ cup (180 ml) of heavy cream until it starts to bubble around the edges. **Then**, pour the hot cream over ½ cup (157 g) of bittersweet chocolate chips and stir until everything is well combined. Spoon the ganache over the cake.

Bake the cake. Evenly divide the batter among the prepared cake pans. Give the pans a gentle tap to remove any air bubbles, then place them on the middle rack of the oven. Bake for 20 to 30 minutes, or until a cake skewer or toothpick comes out clean. Once finished, remove the cakes from the oven and let them sit in the pan for 1 minute before gently inverting them onto cooling racks. Allow the cakes to cool completely before filling and frosting. If you plan to frost later, you can wrap the cakes in plastic wrap and place them in the refrigerator or freezer.

Make the German chocolate frosting. Preheat the oven to 350°F (175°C). Toast the pecans on a baking sheet for about 5 minutes, until fragrant. Once done, remove the baking sheet from the oven and let the pecans cool completely before using them in the frosting. **Next,** in a large bowl, whisk together the evaporated milk, brown sugar, egg yolks, salt and cooled butter until the mixture is smooth. Microwave the mixture in 30-second intervals, stirring every 30 seconds, until it has a thick, dulce de leche–like consistency that coats the back of a spoon. Check for doneness using an instant-read thermometer: The temperature should be 190°F (88°C). Add the vanilla, toasted pecans and sweetened coconut. Mix well. Let the frosting cool completely before spreading it on the cake.

Assemble the layer cake. Make sure the cakes are leveled with a serrated knife if necessary. Apply a small amount of frosting to the bottom of an 8-inch (20-cm) cake board and place the first cake layer on top. Apply a generous amount of frosting to the first layer and spread it evenly with an offset spatula, repeating this process with the remaining cake layers. Store the cake in the refrigerator until ready to serve. Leftovers can be stored in an airtight container in the refrigerator for up to 3 days.

Boston Cream Pie

♣ Makes two 8-inch (20-cm) layer cakes ♣

Boston cream pie is a classic American dessert that has been enjoyed since the nineteenth century. Despite its name, it's actually a cake, not a pie. The dessert is made with two layers of hot milk sponge cake filled with pastry cream and topped with chocolate ganache. Making Boston cream pie can seem intimidating, especially when it comes to making the pastry cream. In this recipe, the process of making the pastry cream has been made effortless with an easy, quick method of making it in the microwave. This moist, decadent dessert is just perfect for any occasion, from birthdays to dinner parties.

Pastry Cream

1¾ cups (410 ml) whole milk

¼ cup (60 ml) half-and-half

6 large egg yolks, at room temperature

½ cup (100 g) granulated sugar

⅓ cup (43 g) cornstarch

5 tbsp (70 g) unsalted butter, cold

2 tsp (10 ml) good-quality pure vanilla extract or 1 vanilla bean, split lengthwise and seeds scraped

Hot Milk Sponge Cake

2½ cups (300 g) cake flour (page 191 or store-bought)

1½ tsp baking powder

¾ tsp salt

1 cup (240 ml) whole milk, at room temperature

¼ cup (55 g) unsalted butter, softened

3 tbsp (45 ml) grapeseed or vegetable oil

1 tbsp (15 ml) good-quality pure vanilla extract

Make the pastry cream. In a 2-quart (1.9-L) glass measuring bowl, whisk together the milk, half-and-half, egg yolks, sugar and cornstarch until the mixture is smooth using a whisk. Then, microwave the mixture on high in 30-second intervals for 5 to 7 minutes, stirring every 30 seconds. After 5 minutes you will notice the thickening of the pastry cream. At 6 minutes you will find that the pastry cream will have a thick and glossy custard-like consistency. Strain the mixture into a medium bowl, add the butter and vanilla. Using a whisk mix until smooth. Cover the bowl with plastic wrap, making sure the wrap touches the surface of the pastry cream and refrigerate until ready to use.

Prepare to bake. Preheat the oven to 325°F (165°C) with a rack in the middle. Spray two 8-inch (20-cm) pans with nonstick cooking spray only on the bottoms and line with parchment paper, leaving the sides untouched.

Sift the dry ingredients. In a medium bowl, sift the cake flour, baking powder and salt (dry ingredients).

Make the hot milk mixture. To prepare the milk mixture, combine the milk, butter and oil in a 4-cup (960-ml) microwave-safe measuring cup and heat in 30-second increments until the temperature reaches 140°F (60°C). Add the vanilla to the hot milk mixture, cover the bowl and let it cool slightly before using (hot milk mixture).

(continued)

Boston Cream Pie (continued)

4 large eggs, at room temperature

2 cups (400 g) granulated sugar

Ganache

¼ cup (60 ml) heavy whipping cream, cold

1 tbsp (15 ml) corn syrup (optional)

4 oz (113 g) bittersweet chocolate, chopped

Beat the eggs and sugar to stiff peaks and prepare the cake batter. In a large bowl, using a hand mixer or a stand mixer with a whisk attachment, beat the eggs and sugar on low speed for 1 to 2 minutes, until frothy. Increase the speed and beat on high for 7 minutes *(egg mixture)*. With the mixer on low speed, gradually add the hot milk mixture to the egg mixture and mix thoroughly *(cake batter)*. **Finally,** fold in the dry ingredients gently in batches of two to the cake batter. The batter will bubble up like pancake batter.

Bake the cake. Divide the batter equally between the prepared cake pans. Tap the pans gently to remove any air bubbles and bake for 23 to 33 minutes, or until a cake skewer or toothpick inserted into the center of the cake comes out clean. Once done, remove the cakes from the oven and let them cool in the pan. Allow the cakes to cool completely before frosting. If you plan to frost later, wrap the cakes in plastic wrap with the pan and store them in the refrigerator. It's best to assemble and frost the cake the day it is served.

Assemble the layer cake. Take the chilled pastry cream from the refrigerator and whisk the pastry cream until it reaches a smooth, custard-like consistency. Apply a small amount of it on the bottom of an 8-inch (20-cm) cake board and place the first cake layer on top. Spread the pastry cream evenly with an offset spatula, then place the second layer on top. It's important to keep the cake chilled in the refrigerator until the ganache is ready.

Make the ganache. Heat the heavy cream and corn syrup in a small, microwave-safe glass measuring cup until it starts to bubble around the edges. Place the chocolate in a small bowl and pour the hot cream over the chocolate. Stir until everything is well combined. Spoon the ganache over the cake with an offset spatula, making sure it's evenly spread over the top of the cake. Once the cake is topped with ganache, store it in the refrigerator until serving. Leftovers can be stored in an airtight container in the refrigerator for up to 3 days. Let the cake rest at room temperature for at least 30 minutes before serving.

Christmas Rum Fruitcake

♣ Makes one 9-inch (23-cm) cake ♣

Boozy Christmas fruitcake is a well-known and loved dessert that is a must-have during the Christmas season, especially in Kerala where it is a staple during the holiday season. The cake is dense and filled with an assortment of nuts and dried fruits that are soaked in rum for several weeks to infuse them with the flavors of the alcohol. Traditionally, black treacle is used to give the cake its distinctive dark color and deep flavor. In this recipe, blackstrap molasses is used as a substitute; it adds a similar depth of flavor while still keeping the cake moist and delicious. To make this cake, the fruits and nuts are soaked in rum for at least two days, but you can soak them for longer if you prefer a stronger boozy flavor. This rich, indulgent dessert is a true holiday classic that is sure to delight everyone who tries it.

Rum-Soaked Fruits

4 cups (480–580 g) dried fruit, such as raisins, sultanas, dried currants and dried cranberries (see Tip)

½ cup (120 ml) dark rum, brandy or fresh orange juice, plus more for feeding the fruit

Cake

2 cups (250 g) all-purpose flour

½ tsp baking powder

½ tsp ground cinnamon

½ tsp ground ginger

½ tsp salt

½ cup (112 g) unsalted butter, softened

1 cup (225 g) packed dark brown sugar

4 large eggs, at room temperature

½ cup (120 ml) grapeseed or vegetable oil

½ cup (170 g) blackstrap molasses or black treacle

1 tbsp (15 ml) good-quality pure vanilla extract

1 tbsp (20 g) apricot preserves

½ cup (64 g) mixed cashews and walnuts, chopped and tossed in 1 tsp flour

1 cup (75 g) candied fruit peel, chopped and tossed in 1 tsp flour

Make the rum-soaked fruits. Place the dried fruits in a glass container with a lid. Pour in enough rum to cover them completely and then seal the container. Let the fruits soak for at least 2 days, though they can be preserved for up to 6 months or longer if desired. Shake the container every other day and add more rum as needed to keep the fruits fully immersed *(rum-soaked fruits)*.

Prepare to bake. Preheat the oven to 350°F (175°C) with a rack in the middle. Spray a 9-inch (23-cm) springform pan with nonstick cooking spray and line the bottom and the sides of the pan with parchment paper. Set it aside.

Sift the dry ingredients. In a medium bowl, sift the flour, baking powder, cinnamon, ginger and salt *(dry ingredients)*.

Beat the fats and sugar. First, use a hand mixer or stand mixer with a paddle attachment to beat the butter and brown sugar until it becomes light and fluffy, which should take around 4 to 5 minutes. Scrape down the sides and the bottom of the bowl with a rubber spatula as needed. **Then,** add one egg at a time, making sure to scrape the bowl in between each addition, and beat until all the eggs are fully incorporated into the batter. Add the oil, molasses, vanilla and the apricot preserves. Mix until well combined. **Next,** add the dry ingredients to the batter in batches of two, mixing until it is just combined. Be careful not to overmix the batter. **Finally,** fold in the soaked dried fruits, nuts and candied fruit peel, ensuring that they are well distributed throughout the cake batter.

(continued)

Christmas Rum Fruitcake (continued)

1 tbsp (8 g) confectioners' sugar, for dusting

> ## Tip
> I used raisins, sultanas, dried cherries, dried cranberries, dried currants and dried apricots, but feel free to use your own favorite dried fruit!

Bake the cake. Scrape the batter into the prepared cake pan and bake for 50 to 60 minutes, or until a cake skewer or toothpick inserted into the center of the cake comes out clean. Once done, remove the cakes from the oven and let them cool in the pan. Allow the cakes to cool completely in the pan for 5 minutes before inverting onto a cooling rack to slice. Once the cake is at room temperature, dust it with confectioners' sugar. Store the cake slices in an airtight container for up to 1 week at room temperature.

Easy Pavlova

♣ Makes one 7-inch (18-cm) pavlova ♣

Pavlova is a beautiful dessert that is perfect for any occasion, especially during the summer months. The key to making a perfect pavlova is in the meringue. It is important to use a clean bowl and whisk attachment, and to slowly add the sugar to the egg whites to create a thick and glossy meringue. Once the meringue is ready, it is shaped into a nest-like form and baked in the oven until it is crisp and dry on the outside. One of the most popular toppings for pavlova is a tangy and sweet lemon curd. While making lemon curd can be a tedious and time-consuming process, the recipe for the curd used in this pavlova is made entirely in the microwave. This means that you can whip up a batch of lemon curd in just a few minutes without having to worry about using a double boiler or constantly stirring the mixture.

Pavlova

6 large egg whites, at room temperature

½ tsp cream of tartar

1 tsp white vinegar

A pinch of salt

1½ cups (338 g) caster sugar (see Tip)

2 tbsp (16 g) cornstarch

1 tsp good-quality pure vanilla extract

Tip

For the best results, I suggest using C & H Baker's Ultra Fine Pure Cane Sugar. Alternatively, you can make caster sugar at home by pulsing or blending granulated sugar a couple of times until it reaches a finely ground consistency. Avoid over-processing it into a powdery texture.

Prepare to bake. Preheat the oven to 275°F (140°C) with a rack in the middle. Trace a 7-inch (18-cm) circle on a parchment paper. Place the paper drawn side down on a baking sheet and set it aside.

Make the meringue. To make a perfect meringue, it is crucial to have a clean stand mixer bowl with a whisk attachment or a hand mixer. Before starting, wipe the bowl with a little vinegar to ensure it's completely clean. **First,** add the egg whites, cream of tartar, white vinegar and salt to the bowl. Mix on high speed for about 4 minutes, until stiff peaks form. **Then,** once the stiff peaks form, it is important to *gradually add the sugar* to the mixture. It is recommended to add the sugar ¼ cup (56 g) at a time and not all at once, while continuously mixing for 6 to 7 minutes with the mixer on high speed. This slow addition of sugar helps to create a thick and glossy meringue with a soft, marshmallow-like texture. **Finally,** sift the cornstarch over the meringue and use a rubber spatula to carefully fold it in until it is fully combined. Add the vanilla and fold gently until everything is mixed.

(continued)

Easy Pavlova (continued)

Lemon Curd

6 egg yolks, at room temperature

1 cup (200 g) granulated sugar

¾ cup (180 ml) lemon juice

Zest of 1 lemon

9 tbsp (126 g) unsalted butter, melted and cooled

Whipped Cream

1½ cups (355 ml) heavy whipping cream, cold

½ cup plus 2 tbsp (76 g) confectioners' sugar

1 tsp good-quality pure vanilla extract

For Assembly

1 cup (125 g) fresh raspberries, for topping

¼ cup (30 g) confectioners' sugar, for dusting

Bake the pavlova. Spread the meringue onto the prepared baking sheet and use an offset spatula to shape it into a nest, creating nice lines from the bottom to the top of the pavlova for a rustic look. Make a well in the center, like a volcano, so that the pavlova cracks evenly in the middle. Place the pavlova on the middle rack and bake for 1 hour 35 minutes. After baking, turn off the oven and leave the door closed for about 3 hours with the oven light on. This slow cooling process helps prevent cracking in the meringue, so it's important not to open the oven door during this time. You can leave the pavlova in the oven with the door closed and the oven light on for up to 24 hours before serving. Once assembled, serve immediately.

Place the mixing bowl with the whisk/beaters in the refrigerator. Chill a mixing bowl and whisk/beaters in the refrigerator for the whipped cream frosting. It's important to keep the mixing bowl very cold to achieve the desired consistency.

Make the lemon curd. Whisk the egg yolks and sugar in a 2-quart (1.9-L) microwave-safe bowl until well combined. Add the lemon juice, zest and cooled butter. Whisk together until thoroughly combined. Microwave the mixture on high for 30-second intervals for about 8 to 10 minutes, stirring after each interval, until it thickens enough to coat the back of a metal spoon. To check for doneness by using an instant-read thermometer: When the internal temperature of the curd reaches 215°F (102°C), it is fully cooked. Strain the lemon curd through a fine-mesh sieve into a glass bowl to remove any cooked bits of egg. Cover the bowl with plastic wrap, ensuring that the wrap touches the surface of the curd to prevent a skin from forming. Refrigerate the lemon curd until you're ready to use it.

Make the whipped cream. In a chilled mixing bowl, combine the heavy cream, confectioners' sugar and vanilla. Beat on medium speed for 1 minute, then increase the speed to high and beat for 4 to 6 minutes, until stiff peaks form.

Assemble the pavlova. Place the pavlova on a serving plate. Spoon and spread a layer of whipped cream on top of the pavlova, spreading it to the edges. **Next,** spoon the lemon curd on top of the whipped cream and spread it evenly. **Finally,** arrange fresh raspberries on top of the lemon curd and dust the whole dessert with a light layer of confectioners' sugar. Serve immediately.

Cream Puffs

♠ Makes 20 to 22 puffs ♠

Cream puffs are light, airy and delicious. This classic French pastry is made from a simple dough called choux pastry, which is baked until it puffs up, creating a hollow center. The filling is usually a rich, creamy pastry cream or whipped cream. Making cream puffs at home may seem daunting, but the process is actually quite simple. The dough is cooked on the stovetop until it forms a ball, and then the eggs are added one at a time to create a smooth, shiny dough. The dough is then piped onto a baking sheet and baked until golden brown and puffy. In this recipe, the choux pastry is partially made in the microwave instead of the traditional stovetop version, making the recipe much easier for bakers of any level to try. The pastry cream filling is made entirely in the microwave, eliminating the need for a stovetop custard.

Pastry Cream

¾ cup (180 ml) whole milk

¼ cup (60 ml) half-and-half

3 large egg yolks, at room temperature

¼ cup (50 g) granulated sugar

2½ tbsp (27 g) cornstarch

2 tbsp (28 g) unsalted butter, cold

1 tsp good-quality pure vanilla extract

Choux Pastry

¾ cup (180 ml) water

¼ cup (60 ml) whole milk

½ cup (113 g) unsalted butter, softened

2 tbsp (26 g) granulated sugar

¼ tsp salt

1¼ cups (150 g) bread flour

Make the pastry cream. In a 2-quart (1.9-L) glass measuring bowl, whisk together the milk, half-and-half, egg yolks, sugar and cornstarch until the mixture is smooth. Then, microwave the mixture on high, in 30-second intervals for 2 to 3 minutes, stirring every 30 seconds. At 2 minutes 30 seconds, the pastry cream will have a thick and glossy custard-like consistency. Strain the mixture into a medium bowl and add the butter and vanilla. Whisk it together until smooth. Cover the bowl with plastic wrap, making sure the wrap touches the surface of the pastry cream and refrigerate until ready to use.

Prepare to bake. Preheat the oven to 425°F (220°C). Line a large sheet pan with parchment paper and set it aside. Chill a mixing bowl and whisk/beaters in the refrigerator for the cream filling. It's important to keep the mixing bowl very cold to achieve the desired consistency.

Make the choux pastry dough. In a large, microwave-safe bowl, combine the water, milk, softened butter, sugar and salt. Microwave the bowl in 30-second intervals, until the temperature reaches 210°F (99°C), or until the mixture froths up and boils. Once the temperature is reached, take the bowl out of the microwave and add the bread flour all at once. Stir vigorously with a wooden spoon until all the flour is incorporated. Place the bowl back in the microwave and microwave for 30 seconds. Remove the bowl and continue to stir the dough until it starts to pull away from the sides of the bowl *(dough)*.

(continued)

Cream Puffs (continued)

4–5 large eggs, at room temperature

Egg Wash
1 egg
1 tbsp (15 ml) milk or cream

Whipped Cream
2 cups (480 ml) heavy whipping cream, cold

½ cup plus 2 tbsp (76 g) confectioners' sugar, plus more for serving

1 tsp good-quality pure vanilla extract

Finish the choux pastry. Scrape the dough into the bowl of a stand mixer or a mixing bowl if using a hand mixer, fitted with a paddle attachment. Beat the dough at a medium speed for 2 minutes to cool it down, although it will still be warm. While the mixer is running, add four eggs, one at a time, stopping to scrape down the sides of the bowl between each addition. Mix until the dough is glossy and smooth, and the eggs are fully incorporated. The dough should be thick and fall slowly and steadily from the beater when lifted out of the bowl. If the dough is still sticking to the beater, add the remaining egg and mix until fully incorporated.

Bake the cream puffs. First, transfer the dough to a pastry bag fitted with a large round tip and pipe dollops that are roughly 2 inches (5 cm) in diameter and 1 inch (2.5 cm) high onto a lined baking sheet. Lightly wet your finger and tap down the spike on top of each dollop. Lightly beat the egg and milk to make an egg wash and brush the tops using a pastry brush. **Then,** bake the puffs in the oven at 425°F (220°C) for about 15 minutes and reduce the temperature to 350°F (175°C) and bake for 15 minutes, or until they turn golden brown and appear dry. Do not open the oven door during the initial baking process to ensure that the puffs rise properly.

Crack open the oven door for 20 minutes. **Finally,** remove the baking sheet from the oven and let the puffs cool completely on it before filling. Once completely cooled, the puffs can be stored in an airtight container at room temperature for 3 to 4 days before assembling.

Make the cream filling for the puffs. In the chilled mixing bowl, combine the heavy cream, confectioners' sugar and vanilla. Using the chilled beaters, beat the mixture on medium speed for 1 minute then increase the speed to high and beat for 4 to 6 minutes, until stiff peaks form. Once the whipped cream is ready, remove the chilled custard from the fridge and whisk it to break it up and smooth out its texture. **Next,** gently fold the whipped cream into the custard until they are well combined. This will create a light and airy filling.

Assemble the cream puffs. Once the filling is ready, transfer it to a piping bag fitted with a star tip. Using a serrated knife, cut the tops off the cooled puffs and pipe the cream filling into each pastry and place the cap on top. Lightly dust the cream puffs with confectioners' sugar. Cream puffs are best when consumed within a few hours of assembly. Store any leftovers in an airtight container in the fridge for up to 2 days.

French Canelés

♠ Makes 14 canelés ♠

French canelés are a delicious pastry that has been popular in France for centuries. Although they require some time and effort, making these canelés at home is not overly challenging. Traditionally, they are made with copper molds and were quite expensive. However, this recipe uses a carbon steel canelé pan, making it a lot easier and less expensive to make at home. Unlike traditional canelés, this recipe does not require any beeswax either, making it much more approachable for bakers. To make these delectable pastries, you will need a few simple ingredients. The batter is mixed and then chilled in the refrigerator for at least two days to allow the flavors to meld and create the signature custardy interior of the canelés. Once the batter has chilled, it is poured into the prepared canelé pan and baked at a high temperature for a short time, and then at a lower temperature for a longer time. This creates a crispy, caramelized exterior and a soft, custardy interior that is simply irresistible.

½ cup (113 g) unsalted butter, softened

1 cup (240 ml) whole milk

1 cup (240 ml) half-and-half

1 vanilla bean, split lengthwise, seeds scraped

1 cup (200 g) granulated sugar

2 large eggs, at room temperature

3 large egg yolks, at room temperature

1 cup (125 g) all-purpose flour

1 tsp rum extract

Prepare the milk mixture. Two days before you plan to make the canelés, combine the butter, milk, half-and-half, vanilla seeds and the vanilla bean in a 4-cup (960-ml) microwave-safe measuring cup. Microwave the mixture on high in 30-second intervals for 4 to 5 minutes, stirring every 30 seconds, until it reaches a boil and the temperature on the thermometer reads 180° to 185°F (82° to 85°C). Once the mixture has boiled, remove it from the microwave and set it aside to cool slightly *(milk mixture)*.

Make the egg-flour mixture. In a separate large bowl, whisk together the sugar, eggs and egg yolks using a whisk very lightly. Avoid incorporating any air into the batter. **Next,** add the flour to the mixture and mix gently until the batter becomes smooth and well combined *(egg-flour mixture)*.

Mix the ingredients and prepare the batter. Remove the vanilla pod from the milk mixture and set it aside. Slowly pour one-third of the warm milk mixture into the egg-flour mixture while whisking quickly to prevent the eggs from cooking. Gradually add the rest of the milk mixture and whisk together until the batter is smooth and similar in consistency to crepe batter. Add the rum extract and strain the batter through a fine-mesh sieve into a large bowl with a spout for easy pouring. Return the vanilla pod to the batter. Cover the bowl with plastic wrap, ensuring that the wrap is in contact with the surface of the batter and refrigerate for at least 2 days.

(continued)

French Canelés (continued)

2 tbsp (28 g) unsalted butter, softened for the pan

Equipment
Carbon steel canelé pan

Prepare to bake. Preheat the oven to 500°F (260°C). Use a pastry brush to coat the canelé pan with softened butter. Place the canelé pan on a baking sheet inside the preheated oven for 5 minutes, until it becomes hot.

Bake the canelés. After removing the batter from the refrigerator, quickly give it a gentle whisk and pour it into the hot molds, filling them not more than three-quarters of the way. It's very important to only fill the molds three-quarters of the way and not to the brim. Place the baking sheet back into the oven and bake for 10 minutes. Then, reduce the oven temperature to 425°F (220°C) and bake for 40 minutes, or until the canelés are dark brown. Remove the baking sheet from the oven and allow the canelés to cool in the molds for 3 to 5 minutes before gently removing them from the molds. Let them cool completely. This pan makes 12 canelés at a time, but the recipe makes 14 canelés. When you make the second batch of two canelés, you will have to reduce the bake time. Bake them at 500°F (260°C) for 10 minutes, then reduce the oven temperature to 425°F (220°C) and bake them for an additional 25 to 27 minutes. These delectable treats can be made ahead of time and frozen in a ziplock bag for up to 1 month. To reheat, place them in a 300°F (150°C) oven for 10 minutes, until they become crispy.

Tips
The batter needs to rest for at least 48 hours.

Fill each mold only three-quarters of the way full with batter and not to the brim.

Make sure to place the canelé pan on a baking sheet before placing it in the oven.

Green Nut Cake

♣ Makes two 9 × 13-inch (23 × 33–cm) sheet cakes ♣

The green nut cake is not just any cake, it's my childhood favorite and it brings back so many cherished memories. I drew inspiration from the iconic cake from Chennai's McRennett Bakery and put my own spin on it using a pistachio sponge cake layered with pistachio cream—a heavenly combination! The pastry cream for this cake is made simple by preparing it entirely in the microwave. Whether it's a special occasion or just a sweet treat, this cake is sure to be a hit with pistachio lovers.

Pastry Cream

1¾ cups (410 ml) whole milk

¼ cup (60 ml) half-and-half

6 large egg yolks, at room temperature

½ cup (100 g) granulated sugar

¼ cup (32 g) cornstarch

5 tbsp (70 g) unsalted butter, cold

2 tsp (10 ml) good-quality pure vanilla extract

Pistachio Sponge Cake

1 cup (120 g) cake flour (page 191 or store-bought)

1 tsp baking powder

¼ tsp salt

6 large egg yolks, at room temperature

1 cup (200 g) granulated sugar, divided

½ cup (120 ml) whole milk, at room temperature

¼ cup (60 ml) olive, avocado or vegetable oil

1 tbsp (15 ml) good-quality pure vanilla extract

¼ cup (78 g) pistachio paste or butter

6 large egg whites, at room temperature

½ tsp cream of tartar

Make the pastry cream. In a 2-quart (1.9-L) glass measuring bowl, whisk together the milk, half-and-half, egg yolks, sugar and cornstarch until the mixture is smooth. **Then,** microwave the mixture on high in 30-second intervals for 5 to 7 minutes, stirring every 30 seconds. After 5 minutes 30 seconds, you will notice the thickening of the pastry cream. At 6 minutes 30 seconds, you will find the pastry cream has a thick and glossy custard-like consistency. Strain the mixture into a medium bowl. Add the butter and vanilla and combine using a whisk until smooth. Cover the bowl with plastic wrap, making sure the wrap touches the surface of the pastry cream, and refrigerate until ready to use.

Prepare to bake. First, chill a mixing bowl and whisk/beaters in the refrigerator for the pistachio cream frosting. It's important to keep the mixing bowl very cold to achieve the desired consistency. **At the same time,** preheat the oven to 350°F (175°C) with a rack in the middle. Spray two 9 × 13 × 0.75-inch (23 × 33 × 1.5–cm) sheet pans with nonstick cooking spray and line the bottoms of the pans with parchment paper.

Mix the ingredients. First, in a medium bowl, sift the cake flour, baking powder and salt *(dry ingredients)*. **Next,** whisk the egg yolks in another medium bowl until well mixed. Add ½ cup (100 g) of sugar to the bowl and mix well. **Next,** pour in the milk, oil, vanilla and pistachio paste and whisk the mixture until it's smooth. Gently fold in the sifted dry ingredients and set the batter aside *(batter)*.

Beat the egg whites to stiff peaks and fold in the batter. In a large, clean bowl, using a hand mixer, whisk the egg whites and cream of tartar on low speed for 1 to 2 minutes, until frothy. Add ½ cup (100 g) of sugar and beat on high for 7 to 8 minutes, until stiff peaks form. Gently fold the whipped egg whites into the batter in three batches.

(continued)

Green Nut Cake (continued)

Pistachio Cream
1½ cups (355 ml) heavy whipping cream

½ cup plus 2 tbsp (76 g) confectioners' sugar

2 tbsp (39 g) pistachio paste or butter (see Tip)

Simple Syrup Soak
2 tbsp (26 g) granulated sugar

¼ cup (60 ml) water

For Enrobing
1 cup (112 g) dry roasted pistachios, roughly chopped

Tip
For the pistachio butter I highly recommend using Vincente™ Sicilian cream of pistachio nut spread.

Bake the cake. Divide the batter equally between the prepared cake pans. Tap the pans gently to remove any air bubbles and bake for 8 to 10 minutes, or until a cake skewer or toothpick inserted into the center of the cake comes out clean. Once done, remove the cakes from the oven and let them cool in the pan. Allow the cakes to cool completely before frosting. If you plan to frost later, wrap the cakes in plastic wrap with the pan and store them in the refrigerator. It's best to frost the cake the same day it's baked after it cools completely.

Make the pistachio cream frosting. In the chilled mixing bowl, combine the heavy cream and confectioners' sugar. Using the chilled beaters, beat the mixture on medium speed for 1 minute, then increase the speed to high and beat for 4 to 6 minutes, until stiff peaks form. Take the chilled pastry cream out of the refrigerator and whisk it until it reaches a smooth, custard-like consistency. Add the whipped cream to the pastry cream in three batches, folding gently with a spatula until well combined. Gently fold in the pistachio paste to the mixture. The cream may not appear very stiff, but it will set once you frost the cake and chill it.

Make the simple syrup. In a small, microwave-safe glass bowl, microwave the sugar and water for 30 to 60 seconds, until the sugar has melted. Set it aside *(simple syrup)*.

Assemble the layer cake. First, cut four equal-sized rectangles from the two sheet cakes and set aside the excess pieces. The thin rectangles that remain can be combined to form the fifth piece. **Next,** spread a small amount of pistachio cream on the bottom of a rectangular cake board and place the first layer on top. **Then,** brush the simple syrup onto the cake's surface with a pastry brush, and apply a generous amount of frosting, about ¾ cup (180 ml), to the first layer, spreading it evenly with an offset spatula. Repeat this process with the remaining cake layers. Apply a layer of frosting all over the cake with an offset spatula, then use a bench scraper to create a perfect rectangle shape by lightly scraping the sides of the cake. Chill the cake in the refrigerator for at least 1 hour. **Finally,** cover the entire cake with pistachios to finish it off. Leftovers can be stored in an airtight container in the refrigerator for up to 2 days.

ALL OTHER TREATS

Here we have a delectable array of desserts that are sure to satisfy any sweet tooth. From the indulgent Espresso Fudge Brownies (page 139) to the unique Matcha Cheesecake Brownies (page 140), there is a perfect treat for every chocolate lover. For those who prefer fruit-based desserts, this chapter also offers the Easy Apple Tarte Tatin with Puff Pastry (page 152) and the Cardamom–Cranberry Curd Tart (page 149), both of which showcase the flavors of seasonal fruits.

The Malai Kulfi Cream Tart (page 146) is a nod to traditional Indian desserts, while the Pecan Pie Cheesecake (page 155) features a no-water-bath method that removes all intimidation and makes this dessert accessible to even the most novice of bakers. And for those who love the fusion of different cultures, the Pista Barfi Donuts (page 162) and Badhusha Donut Holes (page 161) offer a twist on classic American treats, featuring Indian-inspired flavors.

Whether you're looking to impress guests at a dinner party or simply indulge in a decadent dessert, this chapter has you covered. From the crispy and gooey Jammy Donuts (page 157) to the silky and smooth Rose Milk–White Chocolate Panna Cotta Tart (page 143), this chapter offers a range of textures and flavors to suit any taste. So why not treat yourself to a little something sweet?

Espresso Fudge Brownies

♠ Makes 9 big or 12 small brownies ♠

These decadent brownies are the perfect combination of rich chocolate and bold espresso. The crinkly top and fudgy center make for a melt-in-your-mouth treat that's hard to resist. The espresso enhances the chocolate flavor and gives a slight caffeine kick, making it perfect for coffee and chocolate lovers. These brownies are easy to make and perfect for any occasion. Serve them warm or chilled and enjoy the ultimate sweet indulgence.

½ cup (113 g) unsalted butter

4 oz (113 g) good-quality bittersweet chocolate, chopped (preferably Ghirardelli)

2 tbsp (30 ml) olive, avocado, vegetable or canola oil

½ cup (64 g) all-purpose flour

½ cup (45 g) Dutch process cocoa powder

1 tbsp (6 g) espresso powder

1 tsp kosher salt

3 large eggs, at room temperature

1 cup (200 g) granulated sugar

1 tbsp (15 ml) good-quality pure vanilla extract

¼ cup (30 g) chopped walnuts

Tips

To ensure the best results, be careful not to overmix the brownie batter once you add the dry ingredients.

It's important not to overbake the brownies. The toothpick test should result in a few moist crumbs sticking to the toothpick. It's better to slightly underbake the brownies as they will continue to bake as they cool.

Prepare to bake. Preheat the oven to 325°F (165°C) with a rack in the middle. Spray an 8 × 8–inch (20 × 20–cm) baking pan with nonstick spray. Line the bottom of the pan with parchment paper. Make sure to leave some parchment paper hanging over the sides of the pan for easy removal of the brownies. Place the butter in a medium, microwave-safe bowl and microwave for 30 to 60 seconds, until it is completely melted. Set it aside.

Melt the chocolate. Place the chocolate in a large, microwave-safe bowl. Microwave the chocolate at medium power (50%) for 60 to 90 seconds, stirring every 20 to 30 seconds, until the chocolate is fully melted. Add the melted butter to the melted chocolate. Mix well using a spatula until the butter is fully combined with the chocolate. Stir in the oil and set the mixture aside to cool *(chocolate mixture)*.

Mix the ingredients. First, in a medium bowl, whisk together the flour, cocoa powder, espresso powder and salt *(dry ingredients)*. Set it aside. **Next,** in a separate large bowl, using a hand mixer or a stand mixer fitted with a whisk attachment, beat the eggs and sugar on low speed for 1 minute and increase the speed to high and beat for 5 minutes, until the mixture is pale and doubled in volume *(egg mixture)*. **Then,** slowly pour in the chocolate mixture to the egg mixture and gently fold together using a spatula until fully combined. Add the vanilla *(wet ingredients)*. **Finally,** add the dry ingredients to the wet ingredients all at once, and fold gently using a spatula until no streaks of flour are visible. Stir in the walnuts.

Bake the brownies. Scrape the batter into the prepared pan and bake for 25 to 35 minutes, or until a cake skewer or toothpick inserted into the center shows a few moist crumbs sticking to it. Once done, allow the brownies to cool completely in the pan before slicing. They can be stored in an airtight container at room temperature for up to 3 days, and they freeze well too.

Matcha Cheesecake Brownies

♠ Makes 9 big pieces ♠

Matcha cheesecake brownies are a twist on a classic that is sure to impress. These brownies feature a rich chocolate base with a creamy matcha cheesecake layer swirled on top. The matcha flavor adds a pop of color and provides a subtle earthy and slightly bitter taste that pairs beautifully with the chocolate. These brownies are perfect for any occasion, and they're easy to make, even for beginner bakers. They can be stored in an airtight container in the refrigerator for several days, so they make a great make-ahead dessert to satisfy your sweet cravings any time of the day.

Brownie Batter

½ cup (112 g) unsalted butter

4 oz (113 g) 60% bittersweet chocolate (preferably Ghirardelli)

2 tbsp (30 ml) olive oil

1 cup (200 g) granulated sugar

3 large eggs, at room temperature

1 tbsp (15 ml) good-quality pure vanilla extract

½ cup (64 g) all-purpose flour

½ cup (45 g) Dutch process cocoa powder

½ tsp espresso powder

¼ tsp kosher salt

Matcha Cheesecake Batter

2 (8-oz [226-g] each) boxes cream cheese, at room temperature

¾ cup (150 g) granulated sugar

2 large egg yolks, at room temperature

1 tbsp (15 ml) good-quality pure vanilla extract

1 tbsp (6 g) matcha powder (see Tip)

½ cup (84 g) white chocolate chips, melted and cooled

Prepare to bake. Preheat the oven to 325°F (165°C) with a rack in the middle. Spray an 8 × 8–inch (20 × 20–cm) baking pan with nonstick spray. Line the bottom of the pan with parchment paper. Make sure to leave some parchment paper hanging over the sides of the pan for easy removal of the brownies. Place the butter in a medium, microwave-safe bowl and microwave for 30 to 60 seconds, until it is completely melted. Set it aside.

Melt the chocolate. Place the chocolate in a large, microwave-safe bowl. Microwave the chocolate at medium power (50%) for 60 to 90 seconds, stirring every 20 to 30 seconds, until the chocolate is fully melted. Add the melted butter to the melted chocolate and mix well using a spatula until the butter is fully combined with the chocolate. Stir in the oil and set it aside to cool *(chocolate mixture)*.

Make the brownie batter. Add the sugar to the chocolate mixture and mix well using a whisk. Add one egg at a time, whisking well after each addition. Stir in the vanilla. Add the flour, cocoa powder, espresso powder and salt. Whisk together until the mixture is just combined and no streaks of flour are visible. Set the mixture aside.

Make the matcha cheesecake batter. First, in a large bowl with a hand mixer or a stand mixer fitted with a paddle attachment, beat the cream cheese for about 3 minutes, until it becomes smooth. Stop to scrape the bottom of the bowl with a spatula as needed. **Next,** add the sugar and beat for 2 minutes. **Then,** add the egg yolks and vanilla and beat until the mixture becomes smooth. Sift the matcha powder directly over the batter and beat until it is just mixed in. **Finally,** add the melted and cooled white chocolate and beat for a good 2 to 3 minutes, until the mixture becomes glossy.

(continued)

Matcha Cheesecake Brownies (continued)

1 tbsp (15 ml) very hot water

Tip

For those who don't enjoy the flavor of matcha, it's perfectly fine to leave it out of the recipe.

Prepare the brownies. First, reserve a ¼ cup (60 ml) of the brownie batter. Spread the remaining brownie batter evenly in the prepared pan and add the matcha cheesecake batter on top in a smooth layer using an offset spatula. **Then,** in a small bowl, mix the reserved brownie batter with the hot water to thin it out for swirling. Dot ½ teaspoonfuls of the thinned batter on top of the cheesecake batter, then use a skewer to swirl the brownie batter and create a marble pattern.

Bake the brownies. Bake the brownies for 40 to 50 minutes, or until a cake skewer or toothpick inserted into the center shows a few moist crumbs. After baking, let the brownies cool completely in the pan before slicing and storing them in an airtight container in the refrigerator for up to 3 days.

Rose Milk–White Chocolate Panna Cotta Tart

♠ Makes one 9½-inch (25-cm) tart ♠

This is a delicious dessert that combines traditional Indian flavors: Parle-G® biscuit crust, a popular biscuit in India, along with a creamy white chocolate panna cotta infused with rose milk, a refreshing drink in South India. The tart is easy to make and requires no baking, just chilling in the refrigerator. The crust provides a crumbly, buttery base that complements the delicate floral notes of the panna cotta. Rose milk is a popular drink in South India that is made by blending milk with rose syrup, which gives it a sweet, floral flavor and a distinctive pink color. It is a soothing drink that often is consumed during the hot summer months.

Parle-G biscuits have been a staple in Indian households for more than 80 years. The biscuits are known for their crunchy sweetness flavored with cardamom, making it a perfect base for the rose milk panna cotta. The sweetness of the white chocolate perfectly balances the floral notes of the rose milk, creating a well-rounded flavor profile, making it an elegant summer dessert that is sure to impress!

Parle-G Tart Shell

1½–1¾ cups (120–140 g) Parle-G cookie crumbs (see Tips)

3 tbsp (39 g) granulated sugar

½ tsp cardamom powder (page 188 or store-bought)

½ cup (112 g) unsalted butter, melted and cooled

Rose Milk-White Chocolate Panna Cotta Filling

2 tsp (6 g) unflavored gelatin

6 tbsp (90 ml) cold water

4 oz (113 g) white chocolate

2 cups (475 ml) heavy whipping cream, cold

3–4 tbsp (39–50 g) granulated sugar

2 tbsp (30 ml) rose milk syrup or rose syrup (see Tips)

Bake the tart shell. Preheat the oven to 350°F (175°C). In a large bowl, combine the cookie crumbs, sugar and cardamom with a fork. Add the cooled butter and mix until the mixture resembles wet sand. Carefully press the mixture into a tart pan with a removable bottom, starting with the sides using about one-third to one-half of the mixture, then filling in the bottom to ensure even distribution. Place the tart pan on a baking sheet and bake for 10 to 15 minutes, or until the tart becomes a shade or two darker. Once done, remove the pan from the oven and let it cool completely *(tart shell)* before adding the panna cotta filling.

Make the panna cotta filling. First, bloom the gelatin. Sprinkle the gelatin over cold water in a small bowl and let it stand for 5 minutes. **Next,** chop the white chocolate roughly and place it in a separate large bowl *(white chocolate)*. In a 4-cup (960-ml) microwave-safe measuring cup, combine the heavy whipping cream, sugar and rose milk syrup. Microwave on 1-minute intervals, stirring after each interval, for 3 to 4 minutes, until the sugar dissolves and the mixture is very hot but not boiling. Add the bloomed gelatin to the hot cream mixture and whisk thoroughly *(hot cream mixture)*. **Then,** pour the hot cream mixture over the white chocolate. Whisk together until the chocolate melts and the mixture is smooth. Allow the mixture to cool completely *(panna cotta filling)*.

(continued)

Rose Milk–White Chocolate Panna Cotta Tart (continued)

For Serving (optional)

Fresh fruits of choice

Whipped cream (page 185 or store-bought)

Any other toppings of choice

Tips

You can either make crumbs in a blender or you can crush the biscuits placed in a ziplock bag using a rolling pin.

You can find the rose milk or Rooh Afza® syrup on Amazon, or a cocktail rose syrup works as well.

Assemble and set the tart in the refrigerator. Before assembling the tart, it's important to ensure that both the tart shell and panna cotta filling have cooled completely. Slowly pour ½ cup (120 ml) of the panna cotta filling into the tart shell, then place it in the fridge for 10 minutes to set. After 10 minutes, very slowly fill the tart with the remaining panna cotta filling. Once filled, set the tart in the refrigerator for at least 4 to 5 hours or overnight to allow the panna cotta to set properly.

Garnish and serve the panna cotta. Once it's set, you can garnish the tart with fresh fruits, whipped cream or any other toppings of your choice or you can also leave it plain. It looks beautiful and delicious either way. Leftovers can be stored in the refrigerator in an airtight container for up to 2 days.

Malai Kulfi Cream Tart

♠ Makes five 4-inch (10-cm) tarts ♠

These tarts are inspired by the famous Indian ice cream, *kulfi*, featuring a nut crust filled with delectable malai cream. Kulfi is a popular frozen dessert that is made with milk, sugar and flavorings such as cardamom, saffron or pistachio. It has a rich texture that's denser and creamier than regular ice cream. Kulfi is traditionally prepared by slow cooking sweetened and flavored milk until it is reduced to a thick consistency. It is poured into molds and frozen to make a dessert that is perfect for a hot summer day. This tart perfectly captures the flavors of the traditional kulfi in every bite, taking you down the memory lane with each spoonful.

Almond Pistachio Tart Crust

1½ cups (156 g) almond flour

1 cup (240 g) dry roasted pistachios, ground

¾ cup (90 g) confectioners' sugar

1 tsp cardamom powder (page 188 or store-bought)

A pinch of salt

½ cup (112 g) unsalted butter, melted and cooled

Malai Cream

1 cup (240 ml) whole milk

¾ cup (180 ml) evaporated milk

¼ cup (60 ml) condensed milk

¼ cup (50 g) granulated sugar

4 large egg yolks, at room temperature

¼ cup (32 g) cornstarch

¾ tsp cardamom powder (page 188 or store-bought)

2 tbsp (28 g) unsalted butter, softened

Place the mixing bowl with the whisk/beaters in the refrigerator. Chill a mixing bowl and whisk/beaters in the refrigerator for the malai cream frosting. It's important to keep the mixing bowl very cold to achieve the desired consistency.

Bake the tart shell. Preheat the oven to 350°F (175°C). In a large bowl, combine the almond flour, pistachios, confectioners' sugar, cardamom and salt with a fork. Add the cooled butter and mix until the mixture resembles wet sand. Carefully press the mixture into a mini tart pan with a removable bottom, using about 3 to 4 tablespoons (45 to 60 ml) of the mixture in each tart, start by filling the sides and then filling in the bottom to ensure even distribution. Place the tart pan on a baking sheet and bake for 8 to 10 minutes. Once done, remove the pan from the oven and let it cool completely *(tart shell)* before adding the pistachio cream filling. If your crust puffs up slightly, gently press with the back of the spoon and set it aside to cool completely.

Make the malai cream filling. First, in a 2-quart (1.9-L) glass measuring bowl, whisk together the whole milk, evaporated milk, condensed milk, sugar, egg yolks, cornstarch and cardamom using a whisk until the mixture is smooth. **Then,** microwave the mixture on high in 30-second intervals for 5 to 7 minutes, stirring every 30 seconds, until the malai cream has a thick and glossy custard-like consistency. Check for doneness with an instant-read thermometer: The temperature should be 170° to 180°F (77° to 82°C). Strain the mixture into a medium bowl and add the butter. Using a whisk, combine everything until smooth. Cover the bowl with plastic wrap, making sure the wrap touches the surface of the malai cream and refrigerate it for 1 hour.

(continued)

Malai Kulfi Cream Tart (continued)

¾ cup (180 ml) heavy whipping cream

¼ cup (30 g) confectioners' sugar

1 tbsp (7 g) pistachio flour, for dusting (optional)

Next, in the chilled mixing bowl, combine the heavy whipping cream and confectioners' sugar. Using the chilled beaters, beat the mixture on medium speed for 1 minute, then increase the speed to high and beat for 7 to 8 minutes, until stiff peaks form. Take the chilled malai cream out of the refrigerator and whisk it until it reaches a smooth, custard-like consistency. Add the whipped cream to the malai cream in three batches, folding gently with a spatula until well combined *(kulfi cream)*. Set it aside.

Assemble and set the tart in the refrigerator. First, fill the cooled tart shells with the kulfi cream, using a generous amount. Flatten the tops of the tarts with an offset spatula. Any remaining 2 to 3 tablespoons (30 to 45 ml) of kulfi cream can be used for piping or decoration on top. **Next,** add a sprinkle of pistachio flour. Chill the tarts in the refrigerator for 1 hour before serving. Leftovers can be stored in the refrigerator in an airtight container for up to 2 days.

Cardamom–Cranberry Curd Tart

♠ Makes one 9½-inch (25-cm) tart ♠

The holidays are the perfect time for a showstopping dessert that will impress your guests. This tart begins with a crisp, nutty crust, and it is finished with a creamy, tangy cranberry curd filling. In this recipe, the buttery press-in short crust pastry is simple to make and requires only a fork to mix the ingredients; no food processor needed. The cranberry curd is rich and pairs perfectly with the fragrant addition of cardamom. The combination of flavors and textures in this tart make it a must-try holiday dessert!

Cardamom Short Crust Pastry Tart Shell

1 cup (120 g) cake flour (page 191 or store-bought)

1 cup (104 g) almond flour

1 cup (120 g) confectioners' sugar

2 tsp (4 g) cardamom powder (page 188 or store-bought)

¼ tsp salt

½ cup (112 g) unsalted butter, melted and cooled

2 large egg yolks, lightly beaten with a fork

Cranberry Curd Tart

4 cups (400 g) cranberries

1½ cups (300 g) granulated sugar

½ cup (120 ml) fresh orange juice

4 large egg yolks, at room temperature

½ cup (112 g) unsalted butter, melted and cooled

Bake the tart shell. Preheat the oven to 350°F (175°C). In a large bowl, whisk together the cake flour, almond flour, confectioners' sugar, cardamom and salt using a fork. **Next,** add the cooled butter and mix until the mixture takes on the texture of wet sand. Add the lightly beaten egg yolks and mix with a fork. Gently knead the mixture by hand to form a dough. Press the dough into a tart pan with a removable bottom, starting with the sides and then filling in the bottom to ensure even distribution. Place the tart pan on a baking sheet and bake for 20 minutes. After baking, remove the pan from the oven and gently press down any puffed-up areas with the back of a spoon. Set it aside to cool completely (*partially baked tart shell*).

Make the cranberry puree. In a medium saucepan, combine the cranberries, sugar and orange juice. Heat the mixture over medium heat for 10 to 15 minutes, stirring occasionally, until the cranberries start to pop. Remove the saucepan from the heat and transfer the mixture to a blender. Blend until smooth and strain the mixture into a medium bowl to cool completely (*cranberry puree*).

Make the cranberry curd filling. In a large, microwave-safe bowl, whisk the egg yolks. Add the cranberry puree and the cooled butter to the egg yolks and mix until combined. Place the bowl in the microwave and heat for 2 to 3 minutes, stirring every 30 seconds, until the mixture thickens enough to coat the back of a metal spoon. Strain the cranberry curd through a fine-mesh sieve into a medium glass bowl to remove any cooked bits of egg. Cover the bowl with plastic wrap, ensuring that the wrap touches the surface of the curd to prevent a skin from forming and refrigerate for at least 30 minutes (*cranberry curd*).

(continued)

Cardamom–Cranberry Curd Tart (continued)

Italian Meringue (Optional)

4 large egg whites, at room temperature

½ tsp cream of tartar

1⅓ cups (266 g) granulated sugar

⅓ cup (80 ml) water

1 tsp good-quality pure vanilla extract

Assemble and bake the tart. Use a spoon to fill the tart with the curd mixture and use a spatula to gently flatten the top. Bake for 10 minutes, or until the curd has set. After removing the tart from the oven, allow it to cool to room temperature. Once it has cooled, place the tart in the refrigerator overnight to allow it to fully set. Leftovers can be stored in the refrigerator in an airtight container for 1 to 2 days.

Make the Italian meringue. To make a fluffy meringue, start by beating egg whites with cream of tartar in a clean, grease-free bowl of a stand mixer with the whisk attachment until soft peaks form for about 3 minutes. In a medium, heavy-bottomed saucepan, combine the sugar and water and bring it to a boil while stirring continuously. Use a candy thermometer to measure the temperature of the syrup and let it boil until it reaches 240°F (116°C) without stirring. Immediately start the mixer on medium and pour a thin stream of the sugar syrup down the side of the bowl, without touching the whisk. Pour slowly to avoid splashing the syrup. Increase the speed of the mixer to high and beat for 4 to 5 minutes, until stiff peaks form. Stir in the vanilla and mix. Spoon the meringue over the cooled tart, use the back of a spoon to form peaks and torch it with a blow torch.

Easy Apple Tarte Tatin with Puff Pastry

♠ Makes 1 tarte tatin ♠

Tarte tatin is an elegant dessert that can be made quickly and easily with just a few ingredients. The star of this recipe is caramelized apples flavored with vanilla bean and a warm, aromatic blend of spices. The apples are arranged in a circular pattern in a skillet with the caramel sauce to form a beautifully simple pattern. The puff pastry is then laid over the top before baking until golden brown and firm. Once done, the skillet is inverted onto a plate, revealing the lovely apple arrangement on top. This dessert can be served as is or with a scoop of vanilla ice cream, and it is perfect for any occasion, from a casual dinner party to a fancy celebration.

5 tbsp (70 g) unsalted butter

1½ cups (300 g) granulated sugar

1 tbsp (15 ml) lemon juice

1 vanilla bean, split lengthwise, seeds scraped

¼ tsp ground cinnamon

¼ tsp cardamom powder (page 188 or store-bought)

¼ tsp ground ginger

¼ tsp garam masala (optional)

A pinch of salt

9 or 10 small or 8 medium apples, peeled, cored and halved (I use Granny Smith, Braeburn, Pink Lady or any sweet-tart firm baking apples)

1 sheet puff pastry, thawed

Vanilla ice cream, for serving (optional)

Prepare to bake. Preheat the oven to 375°F (190°C). Line a 9-inch (23-cm) cake pan with the parchment paper. Set it aside. Place the butter in a medium, microwave-safe bowl and microwave for 30 seconds, until it is completely melted. Set it aside.

Simmer the apples with the caramel on a stovetop. To a 9-inch (23-cm) skillet over medium heat, add the sugar and melted butter. Cook for 6 to 9 minutes, until the sugar melts and caramelizes, stirring occasionally to prevent burning. Reduce the heat to low and add the lemon juice, scraped vanilla bean seeds and vanilla bean, cinnamon, cardamom, ginger, garam masala (if using) and salt. Arrange the apples in a circular pattern, cut side up, on top of the caramel. Simmer the apples on low heat until they release their juices and absorb the caramel, about 15 to 20 minutes, carefully turning them to cook evenly.

Arrange the apples onto the prepared pan and bake the tarte tatin. To make the apple tarte tatin, arrange the apple slices, cut side up, in a circular pattern on the bottom of a cake pan. Make sure that they are pressed tightly against each other. Pour the remaining caramel over the apples and top with a circle of puff pastry. Gently tuck the edges of the puff pastry down the sides of the pan. Bake in the oven for 35 to 45 minutes, until the pastry is a golden brown and firm. Remove the tarte tatin from the oven and carefully invert it onto a plate. Serve with a scoop of vanilla ice cream (if using). Leftovers can be stored in the refrigerator in an airtight container for 1 to 2 days.

Pecan Pie Cheesecake

♠ Makes one 9-inch (23-cm) cheesecake ♠

Enjoy the ultimate fall dessert with this cheesecake! Baking a cheesecake with a water bath is a proven technique but it can be intimidating for beginners. To provide an easier and stress-free method, I experimented with a slow, low-temperature bake, ensuring a perfect cheesecake consistency without any cracks. The addition of flour in the recipe helps to prevent any cracks as well. With a graham cracker crust mixed with ground pecans and a creamy, rich filling, all topped with a caramel pecan sauce, this cheesecake is sure to impress. Even beginner bakers can master this stunning dessert!

Graham Cracker Pecan Crust

1½ cups (125 g) graham cracker crumbs

¾ cup (84 g) pecans, finely ground

¼ cup (60 g) packed dark brown sugar

⅛ tsp salt

6 tbsp (84 g) salted butter, melted and cooled

Cheesecake Filling

32 oz (904 g) cream cheese, at room temperature

1½ cups (300 g) granulated sugar

½ cup (125 g) ricotta cheese, at room temperature

¼ cup (60 ml) sour cream, at room temperature

½ cup (120 ml) heavy whipping cream

4 large eggs, at room temperature

1 tbsp (15 ml) good-quality pure vanilla extract

2 tbsp (16 g) all-purpose flour

¼ tsp salt

Make the graham cracker pecan crust. Preheat the oven to 350°F (175°C) with a rack in the middle. Prepare a 9-inch (23-cm) springform pan by greasing it with nonstick spray and lining the bottom with parchment paper. In a medium bowl, mix the graham cracker crumbs, pecans, brown sugar, salt and cooled butter. Spoon the mixture into the prepared pan and press it out into an even layer using the back of a measuring cup.

Bake the crust. Bake for 12 minutes, or until the crust starts to look lightly toasted. Remove the pan from the oven and lower the oven temperature to 250°F (120°C). Allow the crust to cool completely.

Make the cheesecake filling. Mix the cream cheese in a hand mixer or stand mixer fitted with the paddle attachment on medium speed for about 1 minute. Then, scrape down the sides of the bowl and mix for 30 seconds. Add sugar and mix for 1 minute, then scrape down the sides of the bowl again. Mix in the ricotta cheese, sour cream and heavy whipping cream. Beat on low speed until the mixture is smooth. Add the eggs one at a time, scraping down the sides of the bowl after each addition. Stir in the vanilla, then add the flour and salt. Mix for 20 to 30 seconds, until the mixture is well combined.

(continued)

Pecan Pie Cheesecake (continued)

Caramel Sauce

1 cup (225 g) packed dark brown sugar

3 tbsp (42 g) unsalted butter, softened

½ cup plus 2 tbsp (150 ml) heavy cream, at room temperature

1 tsp good-quality pure vanilla extract

1 cup (112 g) pecans, toasted (see Tip)

Tip

To toast raw pecans, place them on a lined baking sheet and bake at 350°F (175°C) for 5 minutes in a preheated oven.

Spoon the filling and bake the cheesecake. Spoon the filling over the cooled graham cracker crust, bake the cheesecake for 2 hours on the middle rack of the preheated oven. If the cheesecake starts browning too quickly, tent it with aluminum foil halfway through baking. To check if it's done, gently shake the pan and see if the center slightly wobbles or use a thermometer to check the temperature, which should read 147°F (64°C). Once done, turn off the oven and slightly crack open the door, leaving the cheesecake to sit in the oven for 1 hour. Remove it from the oven and cool the cheesecake at room temperature. Once cooled, cover and refrigerate the cheesecake for at least 4 hours or overnight.

Make the caramel sauce. When serving your cheesecake, prepare the caramel sauce in the microwave by combining brown sugar, butter and heavy cream in a large measuring cup. Microwave the mixture for 1 minute, stir, then microwave for 30 seconds, being careful as it will bubble up. Once it turns golden caramel in color, remove it from the microwave and stir in vanilla until smooth and uniform in color. Allow the sauce to cool completely. Place the toasted pecans in a medium bowl. Pour the caramel sauce over them, gently stirring to ensure the pecans are coated.

Serve the cheesecake. Use a knife to loosen it from the sides of the springform pan, then remove the rim. **Next,** spoon the caramel pecan topping over the top of the cheesecake, ensuring that it is evenly distributed. **Finally,** use a clean, sharp knife to cut the cheesecake into slices for serving. Leftovers can be stored in the refrigerator wrapped in plastic wrap in an airtight container for up to 3 days.

Jammy Donuts

♠ Makes 12 donuts ♠

Fried jammy donuts are a classic treat that have been enjoyed for generations. These donuts are soft, fluffy and filled with a jam filling that oozes out with every bite. After the rich dough has been proofed and rolled out, it is cut into rounds and deep-fried until golden brown. Once fried to perfection, the donuts are rolled in a blend of sugar and vanilla seeds for a sweet and fragrant coating. The best part about these donuts is the jam filling. These traditional jam-filled donuts are a perfect treat to satisfy your craving for a nostalgic favorite.

Donuts

6 tbsp (84 g) unsalted butter

3 tbsp (45 ml) vegetable oil

3 large eggs, at room temperature

2 large egg yolks, at room temperature

1 tbsp (15 ml) good-quality pure vanilla extract

½ cup (120 ml) whole milk

4 cups (548 g) bread flour, plus more for rolling

3 tbsp (13 g) nonfat dry milk powder

¼ cup (50 g) granulated sugar

2 tsp (8 g) instant yeast

1 tsp salt

Make the butter-oil mixture. Place the butter in a medium, microwave-safe bowl and microwave for 30 to 60 seconds, until it is completely melted. Add oil to the melted butter. Set it aside to cool completely.

Make the egg-vanilla-milk mixture. In a medium bowl, lightly whisk together the eggs, egg yolks, vanilla and milk. Set it aside.

Make the dough. In the bowl of a stand mixer fitted with a dough hook attachment, combine the bread flour, milk powder, sugar, instant yeast and salt. Mix on low speed for 10 seconds, until everything is combined. **Then,** pour in the butter-oil mixture and the egg-vanilla-milk mixture and continue to mix, until a sticky dough forms. **Then,** mix on high speed 15 minutes, until the dough pulls away from the bowl and forms a nice, elastic dough.

Proof the dough. Lightly flour the work surface and transfer the dough. Shape it into a ball and let it rest in a lightly oiled stainless bowl. Cover the bowl loosely with a plastic bag or tea towel and let the dough rest in a warm place for 60 to 90 minutes, until it is puffy but not necessarily doubled in size. You can place the bowl in the oven with the light on to create a cozy environment.

(continued)

Jammy Donuts (continued)

Vanilla Sugar

1 vanilla pod, split lengthwise and seeds scraped

1 cup (200 g) granulated sugar

8 cups (1.9 L) vegetable oil, for frying

Seedless raspberry or strawberry jelly, for filling (see Tip)

Roll and form donut balls. Transfer the dough onto a generously floured surface. Sprinkle flour lightly over the dough and the rolling pin and roll it into a thickness of ½ inch (1.3 cm). Cut the dough using a biscuit cutter into rounds about 3 inches (7.5 cm) in diameter. Gently place the donuts on a baking sheet lined with flour. Once you have cut all the donuts and placed them on the baking sheet, leave the baking sheet uncovered in a warm place, preferably in the oven with the light on, for the second proof for 30 minutes.

Make the vanilla sugar. Combine the scraped vanilla seeds and sugar in a blender until well mixed. Set it aside.

Fry the donuts and coat them in vanilla sugar. In a medium-sized, heavy-bottomed pot, heat 3 inches (7.5 cm) of oil over medium heat until the thermometer reads 350°F (175°C). Prepare a plate with paper towels for draining the fried donuts. Slide a couple of donuts at a time carefully into the hot oil, leaving plenty of room for them to float. Fry for about 2 minutes, until golden brown, then flip to cook the other side. Drain the donuts on the paper towel for 1 minute and coat them in vanilla sugar. Repeat the frying and coating process with the rest of the dough.

Fill the donuts with jelly. After the donuts have cooled for a bit, take a chopstick and gently pierce a small hole in the side of each donut, creating a pocket for the filling. Using a pastry bag fitted with a round tip, fill each donut with about 2 tablespoons (30 ml) of jelly. Leftovers can be stored in the refrigerator in an airtight container for up to 4 days.

Tip

To make homemade jelly for your donuts, combine 1 pound (454 g) of hulled and quartered strawberries, a pinch of salt, ¾ to 1 cup (150 to 200 g) of granulated sugar and 2 tablespoons (30 ml) of fresh lemon juice in a medium saucepan over medium heat. Allow the mixture to come to a simmer and continue to simmer for 20 minutes, or until the mixture has thickened into a strawberry compote. **Next,** create a cornstarch slurry by combining 1 tablespoon (8 g) of cornstarch with 1 tablespoon (15 ml) of cold water. Add the slurry to the simmering strawberry compote and continue to simmer for 2 minutes. **Finally,** transfer the jelly filling to a food processor or blender and puree until smooth. Allow the jelly to cool completely before filling your donuts.

Badhusha Donut Holes

♣ Makes 20 donut holes ♣

My inspiration for creating these baked donut holes came from my dad's love for the Indian sweet, *badhusha*. I set out to capture the essence of this dessert and translate it into a modern, baked treat that everyone could easily make at home. These donut holes perfectly blend classic Indian flavors with a contemporary twist. While traditional badhusha is deep-fried and soaked in sugar syrup, this recipe provides all the deliciousness without the frying. The combination of flour, baking powder and yogurt yields a light, fluffy texture that truly captures the essence of the iconic Indian dessert. The warm and fragrant spices of cardamom and saffron pair beautifully with the sweetness of the sugar syrup glaze. These donut holes are a perfect treat for satisfying your sweet tooth any time of day, and they are sure to become a new favorite.

Badhusha Donut Holes

1 tbsp (15 ml) vegetable oil, for greasing the pan

¼ cup (52 g) ghee (page 190 or store-bought)

1½ cups (188 g) all-purpose flour

½ tsp baking powder

¼ tsp baking soda

¼ cup (50 g) granulated sugar

¼ tsp salt

¼ cup (60 ml) plain nonfat or lowfat yogurt, at room temperature

¾ cup (180 ml) water

Saffron Sugar Syrup

½ cup (120 ml) water

1 cup (200 g) granulated sugar

½ tsp lemon juice

½ tsp saffron

1 tsp cardamom powder (page 188 or store-bought)

Prepare to bake. Preheat the oven to 325°F (165°C) with a rack in the middle. Grease the donut hole pans with oil using a silicone pastry brush and set them aside. Place the ghee in a medium, microwave-safe bowl and microwave for 30 to 60 seconds, until it is completely melted. Set it aside to cool completely.

Mix the ingredients. In a large bowl, whisk together the flour, baking powder, baking soda, sugar and salt until they are thoroughly combined. Create a well in the center of the dry ingredients and pour in the melted ghee, yogurt and water. Gently mix the ingredients to form a batter with a consistency similar to that of pancake batter.

Bake the donut holes. Gently spoon or pipe about 1 tablespoon (15 ml) of the prepared batter into the greased donut pan and bake for 35 to 45 minutes, or until they are pale golden brown or a cake skewer or toothpick inserted into the center comes out clean. Take care not to overbake the donuts. Once baked, remove the pan from the oven and let the donuts cool in the pan for 1 minute before transferring them to a cooling rack to cool completely.

Make the saffron syrup and dip the donut holes. Combine the water, sugar, lemon juice, saffron and cardamom in a 4-cup (960-ml) microwave-safe measuring cup. Whisk the mixture until everything is combined, then microwave for 3 to 4 minutes, until the temperature in the instant-read thermometer reaches 200°F (93°C) or until the sugar is dissolved completely. Once the syrup is ready, dip each donut hole in the hot sugar syrup and place it on a serving plate. Spoon any leftover syrup over the donut holes. Leftovers can be stored in an airtight container for up to 2 days.

Pista Barfi Donuts

♣ Makes 14 donuts ♣

These treats are inspired by pista barfi, a decadent Indian sweet that's typically enjoyed during special occasions or festivals. These beautiful little treats are perfect for your Diwali sweet box!

Khova (Mawa)
1 cup (68 g) nonfat dry milk powder

1 tsp ghee (page 190)

¾ cup (180 ml) heavy whipping cream

Donuts
1 tbsp (15 ml) vegetable oil, for greasing the pan

¼ cup (52 g) ghee (page 190)

1½ cups plus 1 tbsp (188 g) cake flour (page 191 or store-bought)

1 tsp baking powder

¼ tsp baking soda

¼ tsp salt

2 tbsp (14 g) cardamom powder (page 188 or store-bought)

1 cup (200 g) granulated sugar

2 large eggs, at room temperature

1 tbsp (15 ml) rose water

½ cup (156 g) pistachio paste or butter (see Tip)

½ cup (120 ml) sour cream, at room temperature

Rose Glaze
2 tbsp (30 ml) rose water

2 tsp (10 g) ghee, at room temperature (page 190)

6 tbsp (78 g) granulated sugar

For Topping
¼ cup (31 g) raw pistachios, crushed

Make the khova in the microwave. To prepare the khova, use a whisk to combine the milk powder, ghee and heavy whipping cream in a large, microwave-safe bowl. Microwave on high in 30-second intervals for 2 to 3 minutes, stirring every 30 seconds, until the mixture has dried up and formed a solid mass. Once the khova is ready, allow it to cool completely before using.

Prepare to bake. Preheat the oven to 350°F (175°C) with a rack in the middle. Grease two nonstick donut pans with nonstick cooking spray and set them aside. Place the ghee in a medium, microwave-safe bowl and microwave for 30 to 60 seconds until it is completely melted. Set it aside to cool completely.

Mix the ingredients. First, in a large bowl, whisk together the cake flour, baking powder, baking soda, salt, cardamom and sugar until they are fully combined (dry ingredients). **Next,** make a well in the center and add the melted ghee, eggs, rose water, pistachio paste, sour cream and khova to the dry ingredients. **Finally,** use a hand mixer to beat until everything is just combined.

Bake the donuts. Spoon or pipe the batter into the prepared pan and bake for 20 to 30 minutes, being careful not to overbake. Then, remove from the oven and let the donuts sit in the pan for 1 minute before transferring them to a cooling rack to cool completely.

Make the glaze. To prepare the glaze, mix the rose water, ghee and sugar in a 4-cup (960-ml) microwave-safe measuring cup. Heat the mixture in 30-second increments, until the sugar has completely melted. Brush the hot glaze over the donuts and sprinkle the pistachios on top. Leftovers can be stored in the refrigerator in an airtight container for up to 3 to 4 days. Let the donuts rest for at least 1 hour at room temperature before serving. You can also warm them up in the microwave.

Tip
I highly recommend using Vincente™ Sicilian cream of pistachio nut spread.

BREAKFAST
SWEETS & BREADS

This chapter features a delectable collection of breakfast sweets and breads, perfect for starting your day on a sweet note. From the flavorful Banana Quinoa Bread (page 167) and the savory Dilpasand (Indian Mince Pie; page 168) to the unique Appam Waffles (page 174) and the soft Japanese Milk Bread (page 171), there's something for everyone.

The Plum Quinoa Muffins (page 177) and the Blueberry-Almond Breakfast Loaf (page 181) are perfect for a quick on-the-go breakfast or a midday snack, while the Saffron-Mango Kesari Bhath Cake (page 178) is a treat to savor with a cup of tea or coffee. Indulge in the variety of flavors and textures, and elevate your breakfast game with these delightful desserts and bread.

Banana Quinoa Bread

♠ Makes 1 loaf ♠

Banana bread is a classic comfort food and a great way to use up all your overripe bananas. But have you ever tried banana bread with a twist? This is a healthier alternative with the addition of quinoa flour, which adds a nutty flavor and a boost of protein, while the ripe bananas and sour cream keep the bread moist and sweet. The recipe is incredibly easy to prepare with just a fork or whisk to mix everything together. Whether it's summer or winter, this bread is a great way to incorporate healthy nutrients into your daily routine.

2 tbsp (28 g) unsalted butter, melted, for the pan

1¼ cups (157 g) all-purpose flour

¾ cup (93 g) quinoa flour (see Tip)

1 tsp baking powder

1 tsp baking soda

¾ cup (170 g) packed dark brown sugar

¼ cup (50 g) granulated sugar

½ tsp salt

1½ cups (338 g) mashed bananas (very ripe; 4–5 large bananas)

1 tbsp (15 ml) good-quality pure vanilla extract

2 large eggs, at room temperature

12 tbsp (168 g) unsalted butter, melted and cooled

½ cup (120 ml) sour cream or plain Greek yogurt, at room temperature

½ cup (60 g) chopped walnuts

Tip

If you don't have quinoa flour, you can substitute it with an equal amount of all-purpose flour or brown rice flour or oat flour or buckwheat flour.

Prepare to bake. Preheat the oven to 350°F (175°C) with a rack in the middle. Use a silicone pastry brush to coat a 9 × 5–inch (23 × 13–cm) loaf pan with melted butter. Line the bottom of the pan with parchment paper and leave enough excess paper overhanging on the sides for easy removal of the loaf.

Mix the dry ingredients. In a medium bowl, whisk together the all-purpose flour, quinoa flour, baking powder, baking soda, brown sugar, granulated sugar and salt until combined (*dry ingredients*). Set it aside.

Mix the wet ingredients. In a large mixing bowl, use a whisk or fork to mix the mashed bananas, vanilla and eggs. Once well combined, add the cooled butter and continue to whisk together until well combined. **Next,** add the sour cream and mix well to fully incorporate it into the mixture (*wet ingredients*).

Combine dry and wet ingredients. After mixing the wet ingredients, add the dry ingredients to the bowl and gently fold them together with a spatula until there are no streaks of flour left (*batter*). **Finally,** add the walnuts and fold them in gently.

Bake the bread. Spoon the batter into the prepared loaf pan and bake for 40 minutes. **Then,** cover the top of the loaf pan with aluminum foil to prevent overbrowning. Continue baking for 20 to 30 minutes, or until a cake skewer or toothpick inserted into the center comes out clean. Allow the banana bread to rest in the pan for 5 minutes before removing it from the pan and transferring to a cooling rack for slicing. Once completely cool, you can slice the bread and store it in an airtight container at room temperature for up to 3 days. The bread can also be refrigerated and warmed in the microwave, or frozen for longer storage.

Dilpasand (Indian Mince Pie)

♣ Makes one 9-inch (23-cm) pie ♣

Dilpasand is a delectable South Indian treat that is popularly found in the famous Iyengar bakeries. It is an Indian-style mince pie that is filled with a coconut and tutti-frutti filling. Once baked, the dilpasand pastry is golden brown and has a fragrant aroma of cardamom and coconut. The filling is sweet, chewy and slightly crunchy, providing a perfect contrast to the flaky and buttery crust. For many people, including me, dilpasand is more than just a pastry—it's a cherished childhood memory. I remember my dad buying these pastries from the Iyengar bakery every Sunday evening. The aroma of freshly baked pastries would fill the house and the excitement of biting into a warm, crispy pastry filled with sweet coconut and colorful tutti-frutti was unmatched. We enjoyed having them with a cup of chai or coffee. It is a perfect snack for any time of the day and is loved by people of all ages.

Flaky Crust (see Tip)

2½ cups (314 g) all-purpose flour, plus more for shaping

½ tsp salt

11 tbsp (155 g) unsalted butter, softened, divided

¼ cup (52 g) ghee (page 190 or store-bought)

¾ cup (180 ml) cold water

Make the flaky crust. In a mixing bowl, whisk together the flour and salt. Add 4 tablespoons (57 g) of butter and the ghee to the flour and salt and rub until the mixture resembles coarse crumbs. Sprinkle with cold water and knead until the dough comes together. Cover and refrigerate for 30 minutes.

Shape the crust. After 30 minutes, remove the dough from the refrigerator and roll it out into a large rectangle on a floured surface. **First,** spread 2 tablespoons (28 g) of softened butter over the surface and fold the smaller ends to overlap each other, making three layers. Sprinkle flour on the surface over the dough and roll it out again to form another rectangle. Then, spread 2 tablespoons (28 g) of softened butter over the surface, sprinkle flour and fold the opposite ends to overlap each other, again making three layers. Roll it out again. **Next,** spread 2 tablespoons (28 g) of softened butter over the surface, sprinkle flour and fold the opposite ends, forming a rectangle. Roll it out again. **Finally,** spread another 1 tablespoon (14 g) of softened butter over the surface, sprinkle flour and fold the opposite ends, forming a rectangle. Freeze the rolled dough for 30 minutes.

(continued)

Dilpasand (Indian Minced Pie) (continued)

Dilpasand Filling

3 tbsp (42 g) unsalted butter, softened

1½ cups (128 g) unsweetened freshly grated coconut

½ cup (115 g) packed dark brown sugar

1 tsp cardamom powder (page 188 or store-bought)

½ cup (120 g) tutti-frutti

2 tbsp (18 g) raisins

2 tbsp (17 g) raw cashews, chopped

Egg Wash

1 egg

1 tbsp (15 ml) water

Tip

Store-bought puff pastry sheets can be a convenient alternative to making the dough from scratch. Just be sure to follow the package instructions for thawing and handling the pastry, and adjust the baking time and temperature as needed for your recipe.

Make the dilpasand filling. Melt the butter in a medium sauté pan over low heat. Once melted, add the coconut and sauté for 1 minute. Add the brown sugar and mix until just combined, allowing the sugar to remain in granular form. Turn off the heat and remove the pan from the stove. Transfer the mixture to a separate medium bowl. Add the cardamom, tutti-frutti, raisins and cashews. Mix everything well and set it aside to cool completely.

Shape and bake the pie. Preheat the oven to 400°F (200°C) with a rack in the middle. On a floured surface, roll out the puff pastry dough into a ¼-inch (6-mm)-thick rectangle. Cut out one large circle and one small circle. Place the large circle on a lined baking sheet or a pie pan. Add the filling to the center of the circle. Place the small circle over the filling and seal the edges of the pie. Make the egg wash by whisking the egg and water in a small bowl until combined. Brush with egg wash and make a cross in the center using a knife. Bake for 30 to 40 minutes, until the top is golden brown. Slice and serve. Leftovers can be stored in an airtight container for up to 2 days.

Japanese Milk Bread

♠ Makes 1 loaf ♠

Japanese milk bread is a fluffy, lightly sweet bread that is popular in Japan and around the world. The key to its texture is the *tanzhong* starter—a mixture of flour and water that is cooked into a paste and added to the dough. This starter gelatinizes the starches in the flour, making the bread soft and moist. This bread has a wonderfully airy texture with a gentle hint of sweetness, making it ideal for sandwiches, toast or simply savoring by itself.

Tanzhong Starter
3 tbsp (45 ml) cold water

3 tbsp (45 ml) whole milk

2 tbsp (15 g) bread flour

Bread
¼ cup (55 g) unsalted butter

2½ cups plus 2 tbsp (361 g) bread flour, plus more for rolling

¼ cup (17 g) nonfat dry milk powder

½ cup (100 g) granulated sugar

1 tbsp (12 g) instant yeast

1 tsp salt

2 large eggs, at room temperature

½ cup (120 ml) whole milk

2 tbsp (30 ml) heavy whipping cream

Make the tanzhong starter. In a small saucepan, whisk together the cold water, milk and bread flour until there are no lumps left. Place the saucepan over low heat and cook the mixture while whisking constantly for 3 to 5 minutes, until it thickens and the whisk leaves lines on the bottom of the pan.

Make the dough. First, place the butter in a medium, microwave-safe bowl and microwave for 30 to 60 seconds, until it is completely melted. Set it aside to cool completely. **Now,** in the bowl of a stand mixer with the hook attachment, combine tanzhong with all the bread flour, milk powder, sugar, yeast, salt, melted butter, eggs, milk and heavy whipping cream.

Then, mix on low speed for 1 minute, until everything is fully incorporated. **Next,** mix on high speed for 20 to 25 minutes, until the dough becomes elastic and pulls away from the bowl. To test if the dough is ready, use the windowpane method by stretching a small piece of dough between your fingers, it should be thin and translucent.

Rest the dough. Lightly flour a work surface and transfer the dough, shaping it into a ball. Let it rest in a lightly oiled stainless steel bowl, covering it loosely with plastic wrap or a tea towel for 60 to 90 minutes, until the dough becomes puffy, but not necessarily doubled in size. For a warmer environment, you can place the bowl in the oven with the light on.

(continued)

Japanese Milk Bread (continued)

1 tbsp (15 ml) milk, for brushing

Form the shape of the bread. Once the dough has risen, transfer it to a generously floured surface and gently deflate it. Divide the dough into three equal portions and use a lightly floured rolling pin to roll each portion into a thin rectangle, then roll it up into a coil shape. Repeat this process with the remaining two portions.

Place the coils into a lightly greased 9 × 5–inch (23 × 13–cm) loaf pan, with the seam sides facing downward. Cover the pan loosely with plastic wrap and allow it to rest for at least 1 hour, until the dough has risen to almost the top of the pan and is super puffy.

Bake the bread. To bake the loaf, preheat the oven to 350°F (175°C) and brush the loaf with milk. Bake for 30 to 35 minutes, until it's golden brown on top and an instant-read thermometer inserted into the center reads at least 190°F (88°C). Take the loaf out of the oven and allow it to cool in the pan for at least 10 minutes, then transfer it to a cooling rack to cool completely. To store leftover bread, wrap it well and keep it at cool room temperature for 5 to 7 days, or freeze it for up to 1 month.

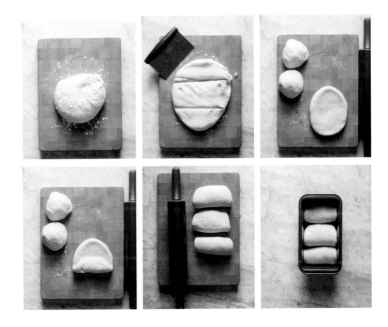

Appam Waffles

♠ Makes 4 or 5 large waffles ♠

These flavor-packed waffles will transport you to the streets of South India! Appam waffles are a creative fusion of traditional South Indian sweet appam or *paniyaram* and classic American waffles. They are made with a combination of all-purpose flour, coconut milk, freshly grated coconut, ghee and banana, with a delicate aroma of cardamom. These waffles are scrumptious and also very easy to prepare, making them a popular breakfast or snack option for both adults and kids.

1 cup (125 g) all-purpose flour or whole-wheat flour

½ cup (79 g) white rice flour

¾ cup (150 g) granulated sugar or powdered jaggery

1 tbsp (7 g) cardamom powder (page 188 or store-bought)

⅛ tsp salt

¼ tsp baking powder

½ cup (120 ml) coconut milk

¾ cup (180 ml) water

¼ cup (52 g) ghee, melted and cooled (page 190 or store-bought)

¾ cup (167 g) mashed bananas or 1 large banana mashed

3 tbsp (18 g) freshly grated coconut, unsweetened

2 tbsp (26 g) ghee, for cooking (page 190 or store-bought)

2 tbsp (16 g) confectioners' sugar, for dusting (optional)

Mix the ingredients. First, in a large bowl, whisk together the all-purpose flour, white rice flour, sugar, cardamom, salt and baking powder until combined *(dry ingredients)*. **Then,** in a separate medium bowl, whisk together the coconut milk and water using a fork *(wet ingredients)*.

Mix the ingredients. Pour the wet ingredients into the bowl with the dry ingredients and whisk together until well combined. **Then,** add the cooled ghee and mix until the batter is thick and smooth. **Finally,** fold in the bananas and coconut. You should have a thick batter.

Cook the waffles. Preheat your waffle maker to medium-high heat (around level 4 or 5). Grease the waffle iron with a few drops of ghee. Add ½ to ¾ cup (120 to 180 ml) of the batter to the waffle iron, depending on the desired size of your waffles. Close the waffle iron and cook until the light turns green or the waffle is golden in color. Once cooked, remove the waffle from the waffle iron and place it on a serving plate. Repeat the process with the remaining batter. To finish, dust the waffles with confectioners' sugar (if using). Leftovers can be stored in the refrigerator in an airtight container for up to 2 days.

Tips

You can swap the sugar in the recipe with equal amounts of jaggery powder to add an earthy flavor to your waffles.

If you're using sweetened coconut flakes, it's recommended that you reduce the total sugar content to ½ cup (100 g).

Plum Quinoa Muffins

♣ Makes 6 jumbo muffins ♣

This delightful muffin has become a family favorite at home, especially for my sweet-toothed kids. They have the same soft texture as bakery-style muffins, and they have the added bonus of being packed with nutrition. One of the best things about these muffins is how easily they can be customized. While the recipe calls for plums, you can easily swap them out for other seasonal fruits, such as apples or pears. Adding a bit of ground cinnamon can also give them a cozy autumn twist. The recipe is simple and easy to follow, making it perfect for beginner bakers. These muffins are sure to be a crowd-pleaser, with their classic domed top and delicious flavor that both kids and adults will love.

1¾ cups (218 g) all-purpose flour

1 cup (124 g) quinoa flour

1 tbsp (14 g) baking powder

½ tsp baking soda

¼ tsp salt

1 cup (200 g) granulated sugar

½ cup (120 ml) vegetable or avocado oil

4 tbsp (57 g) unsalted butter, melted and cooled

2 large eggs, at room temperature

1 tbsp (15 ml) good-quality pure vanilla extract

½ cup (120 ml) sour cream or plain Greek yogurt, at room temperature

3 medium ripe-but-firm plums

Coarse sugar, such as turbinado or demerara, for sprinkling

Prepare to bake. Preheat the oven to 375°F (190°C) with a rack in the middle. Line a jumbo muffin pan with six jumbo paper liners.

Mix the ingredients. First, in a medium bowl, whisk together the all-purpose flour, quinoa flour, baking powder, baking soda and salt *(dry ingredients)* until combined. Set it aside. **Then,** in a large bowl using a hand mixer or a stand mixer fitted with a paddle attachment, beat the sugar, oil and cooled butter for 2 to 3 minutes. Stop to scrape down the sides and the bottom of the bowl with a rubber spatula as needed. Beat in the eggs one at a time until fully incorporated, scraping after each addition. Stir in the vanilla and mix until just combined. **Finally,** at low speed, mix in half the dry ingredients until just combined, then add the sour cream and mix. Add the remaining half of the dry ingredients and mix until just combined, ensuring no streaks of flour remain visible.

Bake the muffins. Divide the batter equally, top each muffin with 2 to 3 slices of plum and sprinkle with coarse sugar. Bake the muffins for 25 to 35 minutes, or until the tops are golden brown and a cake skewer or toothpick inserted into the center comes out clean. Let the muffins cool in the pan for 5 to 10 minutes before serving them warm or at room temperature. You can store the muffins in an airtight container at room temperature for up to 2 days, or refrigerate for up to 1 week and warm them in the microwave later. They also freeze well for up to 1 month.

Tip

Additionally, you can switch up the fruit by swapping plums for apples or pears and add 1 teaspoon of ground cinnamon to give the batter for a cozy autumn twist.

Tip

If you don't have quinoa flour, don't worry! You can still make these muffins by substituting all-purpose flour in a 1:1 ratio. Alternatively, you can use almond flour as a replacement for quinoa flour.

Saffron-Mango Kesari Bhath Cake

♣ Makes one 8-inch (20-cm) cake ♣

This breakfast cake is a baked adaptation of the popular South Indian sweet breakfast dish, *mango kesari baat*. The cake is enriched with the goodness of fresh mangoes and the warm aroma of saffron and cardamom. What sets this cake apart is the coarse texture that is achieved with the use of semolina. The addition of almond flour adds a nutty flavor to the cake, making it an irresistible treat with every bite.

1 cup (167 g) fine semolina or semolina flour

½ cup (52 g) almond flour

1 tsp baking powder

½ tsp baking soda

1 tbsp (7 g) cardamom powder (page 188 or store-bought)

¼ tsp salt

1½ cups (265 g) chopped mango

¾ cup (150 g) granulated sugar

A generous pinch of saffron

¼ cup (60 ml) plain nonfat yogurt, at room temperature

¼ cup (60 ml) olive or avocado oil

Tip

Resting the cake batter is a crucial step as it allows the semolina to absorb all the mango flavors, resulting in a moist and flavorful cake. This also helps prevent the cake from drying out after baking.

Mix the dry ingredients. In a large bowl, whisk together the fine semolina, almond flour, baking powder, baking soda, cardamom and salt until combined *(dry ingredients)*. Set it aside.

Blend the mango, sugar and saffron and mix together all the ingredients. Add the mango chunks, sugar and saffron to a blender. Blend until smooth. Transfer the mixture to the bowl with the dry ingredients. Add the nonfat yogurt and oil to the bowl and whisk together until everything is well combined. Cover the bowl with a plate or plastic wrap and let the batter rest for 20 minutes.

Prepare to bake. Preheat the oven to 350°F (175°C) with a rack in the middle. Spray an 8-inch (20-cm) round pan with nonstick spray. Line the bottom of the pan with parchment paper.

Rest the batter for 20 minutes (see Tip) and bake the cake. Once the batter has rested for 20 minutes, spoon it into the prepared pan and bake it for 25 to 35 minutes, or until a cake skewer or toothpick inserted into the center comes out clean. After baking, let the cake rest in the pan for 5 minutes before inverting it onto a cooling rack to slice. Wait until the cake has cooled completely before slicing it into pieces. Leftovers can be stored in an airtight container in the refrigerator for up to 2 days.

Blueberry-Almond Breakfast Loaf

♣ Makes 1 loaf ♣

This one-bowl breakfast loaf is perfect for busy mornings when you need a quick and easy recipe. All you have to do is mix the ingredients in a bowl, add the blueberries and bake! You can use any type of berries, fresh or frozen. The addition of almond flour gives the bread a nutty flavor and the yogurt keeps it moist. This loaf is delicious and soft with a subtle tang, and it makes for a beautiful addition to your breakfast table, especially during the summer months.

2 tbsp (28 g) unsalted butter, melted, for the pan

1½ cups (233 g) fresh or frozen blueberries (see Tips)

2 tsp (6 g) all-purpose flour, for the blueberries (if using fresh)

1¾ cups (218 g) all-purpose flour

¾ cup (78 g) almond flour

1¼ cups (250 g) granulated sugar

2 tsp (9 g) baking powder

¼ tsp baking soda

¼ tsp salt

1 cup (240 ml) plain Greek yogurt, at room temperature

3 large eggs, at room temperature

1 tsp lemon zest

½ cup (112 g) unsalted butter, melted and cooled

1 tbsp (15 ml) good-quality pure vanilla extract

1 tsp lemon juice

Tips

Frozen blueberries can also be used, without thawing them. Simply mix them in while they're still frozen; no need to toss them in flour.

If you don't have almond flour, you can use all-purpose flour instead, in a 1:1 ratio.

Prepare to bake. Preheat the oven to 350°F (175°C) with a rack in the middle. Use a silicone pastry brush to grease a 9 × 5–inch (23 × 13–cm) loaf pan with melted butter, which can be melted in the microwave and used right away without waiting for it to cool to room temperature. Line the bottom of the pan with parchment paper, making sure to leave some paper hanging over the sides of the pan to make it easy to remove the loaf from the pan later.

Prepare the blueberries. If using fresh blueberries, toss them with 2 teaspoons (6 g) of flour. If using frozen blueberries, skip this step (see Tips).

Mix all the ingredients. In a large bowl, whisk together the all-purpose flour, almond flour, sugar, baking powder, baking soda and salt until well combined. **Next,** create a well in the center of the dry ingredients. Add the yogurt, eggs, lemon zest, cooled butter, vanilla and lemon juice. Whisk together until everything is just combined. Be careful not to overmix the batter.

Fold in the blueberries and bake the bread. Gently fold in the blueberries and spoon the batter into the prepared loaf pan. Bake the bread for 50 to 60 minutes, or until a cake skewer or toothpick inserted into the center comes out clean. Allow the bread to rest in the pan for 5 minutes before transferring it to a cooling rack. Slice it when it is completely cool.

This bread can be stored in an airtight container at room temperature for up to 2 days. It can also be refrigerated for up to 1 week or frozen for up to 1 month.

BASICS & HOW-TO
TUTORIALS

Here is your ultimate guide to making the recipes from this cookbook. With a range of tutorials on glazes, ganache, whipped cream, citrus curd and even how to make your own ghee, cake flour and ground cardamom, you'll have everything you need to create any of the delectable sweets on offer. Along with classic desserts, such as My Mom's Ultimate Trifle (page 187), this section also includes useful tips such as how to brown butter. Whether you're a beginner or an experienced baker, these step-by-step instructions will help you master the art of sweet-making and elevate your baking game.

Glazes

♠ Makes about 1 cup (300 g) ♠

Glazes are an elegant and effortless way to dress up cakes, cookies and other desserts. Making a glaze is easy—all you need to do is whisk together the ingredients and pour it over the dessert. Here you will find recipes for a variety of simple glazes that are quick and simple to make, and they can elevate the flavor and appearance of any dessert. Adjust the amount of liquid if you prefer a thinner or thicker glaze.

Simple Vanilla Glaze

2 cups (240 g) confectioners' sugar

1 tsp good-quality pure vanilla extract

5 tbsp (75 ml) milk or cream

A pinch of salt

Chocolate Coffee Glaze

2 cups (240 g) confectioners' sugar

3 tbsp (18 g) Dutch process cocoa powder

5 tbsp (75 ml) brewed coffee, cold

1 tsp Kahlúa liquor (optional)

Chocolate Glaze

4 oz (113 g) chopped bittersweet chocolate (preferably Ghirardelli)

½ cup (120 ml) heavy whipping cream, cold

2 tbsp (28 g) unsalted butter, softened

Cardamom-White Chocolate Glaze

4 oz (113 g) chopped white chocolate (preferably Ghirardelli)

½ cup (120 ml) heavy whipping cream, cold

2 tbsp (28 g) unsalted butter, softened

½ tsp cardamom powder (page 188 or store-bought)

Make the simple vanilla glaze. Whisk together the confectioners' sugar, vanilla, milk and salt until smooth. Adjust the amount of milk or confectioners' sugar if you prefer a thinner or thicker glaze.

Make the chocolate coffee glaze. Whisk together the confectioners' sugar, cocoa powder, coffee and Kahlúa (if using) until smooth.

Make the chocolate glaze. Place the chocolate in a large bowl. Heat the cream in a medium glass measuring cup in the microwave for 45 to 60 seconds, until hot. Pour it over the chocolate let it stand for 2 minutes. Add the butter and whisk together until smooth. Set it aside and stir occasionally until it is slightly thickened.

Make the cardamom–white chocolate glaze. Place the white chocolate in a large bowl. Heat the heavy whipping cream in a medium glass measuring cup in the microwave for 45 to 60 seconds, until hot. Pour it over the chocolate let it stand for 2 minutes. Add the butter and cardamom. Whisk together until smooth. Set it aside and stir occasionally until it's slightly thickened.

(continued)

Lemon Glaze

2 cups (240 g) confectioners' sugar

1 tsp lemon zest

5 tbsp (75 ml) fresh lemon juice

Rum Glaze

2 cups (240 g) confectioners' sugar

1 tsp rum extract

5 tbsp (75 ml) milk or cream

Cream Cheese Glaze

1½ cups (180 g) confectioners' sugar

2–3 tbsp (30–45 ml) whole milk

1 tsp good-quality pure vanilla extract

3 oz (85 g) cream cheese, at room temperature

Make the lemon glaze. Whisk together the confectioners' sugar, lemon zest and lemon juice until smooth.

Make the rum glaze. Whisk together the confectioners' sugar, rum extract and milk until smooth. Adjust the amount of cream if you prefer a thinner or thicker glaze.

Make the cream cheese glaze. Whisk together the confectioners' sugar, milk and vanilla until smooth. **Then,** add the cream cheese and mix well until the glaze is creamy and fully combined.

Ganache 3 Ways

♠ Makes 2 cups (457 g) ♠

Ganache is a popular and delicious topping for cakes and other desserts. It is made by adding heated cream to chopped chocolate to create a rich, silky mixture. Ganache can be used in various ways: It can be poured over cakes as a glaze, used as a filling for cakes, or whipped to create a fluffy frosting. Making ganache is simple, and you can never go wrong with it.

8 oz (226 g) good-quality bittersweet or semisweet chocolate, chopped (preferably Ghirardelli or Scharffen Berger)

1 cup (240 ml) heavy cream

Make the ganache. Add the chocolate to a large bowl. In a 4-cup (960-ml) microwave-safe glass measuring cup, heat the heavy cream for 60 to 90 seconds, or until it starts to bubble around the edges. **Then,** pour the hot cream over the chocolate and stir until everything is well combined.

Spoon the warm ganache over the dessert for the glaze. Let it cool at room temperature and use it as a filling and frosting for cakes and macaroons. To use it for frosting layer cakes instead of a buttercream, set the ganache bowl covered in plastic wrap in the refrigerator for about 1 hour and then whip it using a hand mixer at high speed until it is light and fluffy.

Whipped Cream 3 Ways

♠ Makes 3½ cups (140 g) ♠

Whipped cream is a delicious and versatile topping that can be used on cakes, pies and other desserts. It's easy to make by whipping heavy cream with sugar and vanilla extract. However, whipped cream can sometimes become unstable, causing it to weep and deflate quickly. To stabilize whipped cream, you can add dry milk powder or gelatin to the mixture. Dry milk powder helps to thicken the cream to keep it stable; gelatin helps to strengthen the structure of the whipped cream. Here are the recipes for whipped cream frosting using both of these methods, so you can create beautiful, stable whipped cream frostings for your desserts.

Whipped Cream

1¾ cups (410 ml) heavy whipping cream, cold

½ cup plus 2 tbsp (76 g) confectioners' sugar

1 tsp good-quality pure vanilla extract

Stabilized Whipped Cream (Milk Powder)

1¾ cups (410 ml) heavy whipping cream, cold

½ cup plus 2 tbsp (76 g) confectioners' sugar

1 tsp good-quality pure vanilla extract

½ cup (34 g) nonfat dry milk powder

Stabilized Whipped Cream (Gelatin)

1 tsp unflavored gelatin

4 tsp (20 ml) water

1¾ cups (410 ml) heavy whipping cream, cold

½ cup plus 2 tbsp (76 g) confectioners' sugar

1 tsp good-quality pure vanilla extract

Place the mixing bowl with the whisk/beaters in the refrigerator. Chill a mixing bowl and whisk/beaters in the refrigerator for the whipped cream frosting. It's important to keep the mixing bowl very cold to achieve the desired consistency.

Make the whipped cream. Using a stand mixer with the whisk attachment or a hand mixer, beat the heavy whipping cream, confectioners' sugar and vanilla on medium speed for 1 minute. Gradually increase the speed to high and beat for 4 to 6 minutes, until stiff peaks form. Make sure not to overbeat the whipped cream as it may turn into butter. Spoon over desserts and serve immediately.

Make the stabilized whipped cream using dry milk powder. To stabilize the whipped cream, using a stand mixer with the whisk attachment or a hand mixer, beat the heavy whipping cream, confectioners' sugar, vanilla and milk powder on medium speed for 1 minute. Gradually increase the speed to high and beat for 4 to 6 minutes, until stiff peaks form. Make sure not to overbeat the whipped cream as it may turn into butter. Pipe or decorate as required.

Make the stabilized whipped cream using gelatin. If you are in a hotter climate and prefer a more stable frosting, you can use unflavored gelatin to stabilize it. **First,** bloom the gelatin in the water in a small, microwave-safe bowl. Set it aside for 5 minutes, then melt it in the microwave for about 5 seconds. Be careful not to overheat it or it may curdle the cream. Cool completely. In a chilled mixing bowl using hand mixers, beat the heavy whipping cream, confectioners' sugar and vanilla on medium speed until soft peaks form. **Then,** drizzle in the melted gelatin mixture while continuing to mix on low speed. Keep mixing until the peaks are firm enough to hold their shape, but be sure not to overmix. Frost as desired.

Citrus Curds

♠ Makes 1½ cups (355 ml) ♠

Citrus curd is an amazing topping for desserts and it can be made with any citrus fruit including tangerines, oranges, lemons, limes and grapefruits. The best part is that it can be prepared completely in the microwave, making it quick and easy. Citrus curd can be used as a topping for cakes, cupcakes, scones and more. It also can be used as a filling for tarts, topping pavlovas or as a layer in a trifle. It's a delicious addition to any dessert.

6 egg yolks, at room temperature

1 cup (200 g) granulated sugar

¾ cup (180 ml) citrus juice

Zest of 1 citrus fruit (same fruit as used for juice)

9 tbsp (126 g) unsalted butter, melted and cooled

Make the citrus curd in the microwave. Whisk together the egg yolks and sugar in a 2-quart (1.9-L) microwave-safe bowl until well combined. Add the citrus juice, zest and cooled butter. Whisk together until thoroughly combined. Microwave the mixture on high for 1-minute intervals for 8 to 10 minutes, stirring after each interval, until it thickens enough to coat the back of a metal spoon. You can also check for doneness by using an instant thermometer. When the internal temperature of the curd reaches 215°F (102°C), it is fully cooked.

Strain the citrus curd through a fine-mesh sieve into a medium glass jar or bowl to remove any cooked bits of egg, then cover the bowl with plastic wrap, ensuring that the wrap touches the surface of the curd to prevent a skin from forming. The curd can be stored in the refrigerator for up to 10 days

My Mom's Ultimate Trifle

This light and comforting trifle is my mom's signature dessert from the 1980s. It's the perfect way to end a heavy meal, and it brings back a lot of nostalgic memories for me. My mom used to use vanilla custard, but I've replaced it with a richer-tasting diplomat cream. The great thing about this recipe is that you can go wild with the fruit and toppings, using any that you have on hand. This trifle starts with a layer of cake, topped with diplomat cream, then a layer of fruits and nuts. Just repeat these layers until the bowl is full! Refrigerate the trifle for a few hours to let the flavors meld, and you have the perfect dessert to impress your guests.

Diplomat Cream

1 recipe vanilla pastry cream (page 133), chilled

1 recipe whipped cream (page 185)

Trifle

1 recipe Brown Butter–Vanilla Pound Cake (page 17)

3–4 cups (weight varies) fresh fruit of your choice

1 cup (weight varies) dry roasted nuts, such as cashews, almonds and pistachios

Make the diplomat cream. Take the chilled pastry cream out of the refrigerator and whisk it until it reaches a smooth, custard-like consistency. Add the whipped cream to the pastry cream in three batches, folding gently with a spatula until well combined.

Make the trifle. First, chop the cake into 1-inch (2.5-cm) cubes to fit the bottom of the trifle bowl or a large clear bowl. Make sure that the entire bottom of the bowl is covered with cake. **Then,** add a layer of the cream, followed by a layer of fruit and nuts. **Repeat** the layers until the bowl is full, ending with a layer of cream on top. The number of layers can vary depending on the size of the bowl and personal preference. Once assembled, refrigerate the trifle for at least 1 hour before serving to allow the flavors to meld.

Homemade Ground Cardamom

♠ Makes 1 cup (112 g) ♠

Cardamom powder is a popular spice that is ground and used in many recipes. While it's easy to buy premade cardamom powder, making it at home can be a more economical and fresher option, and it is a simple way to add a flavorful touch to your cooking and baking. Plus, roasting the cardamom pods beforehand can enhance their natural aroma and flavor, making the homemade powder even more delicious.

1 cup (96 g) green cardamom pods
4 tsp (16 g) granulated sugar

Make the cardamom powder. First, place whole cardamom pods in a *kadai* (a type of Indian frying pan), a flat skillet or a nonstick pan and roast them over low-medium heat. Continue roasting the cardamom pods for 1 to 2 minutes, or until you notice some spots on them and they become aromatic. Once roasted, transfer the cardamom pods to a plate and allow them to cool slightly.

Next, add the slightly warm cardamom pods to a mixer or spice grinder and add the sugar. Grind the mixture until it becomes a fine powder. Once ground, transfer the cardamom powder to an airtight container for storage for up to 2 months at room temperature and up to 6 months in the refrigerator.

Brown Butter

♠ Makes ¾ cup (180 ml) ♠

Brown butter adds a nutty aroma and taste to baked goods. This book includes recipes for a Brown Butter–Vanilla Pound Cake (page 17) and a Brown Butter, Cardamom & Banana Bundt Cake (page 22) that both use brown butter as a key ingredient. Both of these cakes are a testament to the versatility of brown butter in baking. It adds a depth of flavor and richness that can take a classic dessert to the next level. Brown butter is made by cooking butter until the milk solids start to brown. There are two methods to make brown butter—on the stovetop or in the microwave. While both methods will give you delicious brown butter, the microwave method is the easiest and most convenient.

1 cup (225 g) unsalted butter, softened

Make brown butter on the stovetop. Melt the butter in a medium saucepan over medium heat. Stir gently with a rubber spatula or whisk to prevent milk solids from sticking to the bottom of the pan. The butter will start foaming and turning bubbly as it melts. Watch it carefully as it slowly changes color from pale yellow to a tan hue and develops a nutty aroma, about 5 to 8 minutes.

Once it reaches a dark amber brown color, remove it from the heat and pour it into a heatproof bowl to cool. Be sure to remove it from the pan to prevent further cooking and the risk of burning. You can strain the butter to remove any burned bits or leave them to enhance the toasted flavor. Allow the brown butter to cool to room temperature before using it for baking recipes and store the remaining butter in the refrigerator for up to 2 weeks.

Make brown butter in the microwave. In a 4-quart (3.8-L) microwave-safe bowl, place ½ cup (112 g) of the butter and cover it with a microwave-safe plate that fits properly. This step is important as the butter may splash and splatter during the process. Microwave the butter in 30-second intervals for 5 to 8 minutes, stirring every 30 seconds. Keep a close eye on it as it browns. You'll know it's ready when it emits a nutty aroma and turns a dark amber color. Using oven mitts, carefully remove the bowl from the microwave. Transfer the brown butter to another bowl and set it aside to cool completely. Repeat the same process with the remaining ½ cup (112 g) of butter. Once this batch turns dark amber in color, carefully add it to the previous batch and set all of the brown butter aside to cool completely. By browning the butter in smaller batches, you can avoid making a mess in the microwave. Take care while working with the hot butter and ensure it has cooled before using it in your recipe. Store the remaining butter in the refrigerator for up to 2 weeks.

Homemade Ghee

♠ Makes 1½ cups (360 ml) ♠

Ghee is a type of clarified butter that is commonly used in Indian cuisine. It has a rich, nutty flavor and a distinctive aroma that is highly prized in Indian desserts and other dishes. Making ghee at home is a simple, economical way to add this delicious ingredient to your cooking. Always keep the ghee in a cool, dark spot in the pantry for best storage. Properly stored ghee can last up to one year at room temperature. This book features many recipes that use ghee, such as Makkan Peda Cake (page 35), Soan Papdi Cookies (page 76), Cardamom Ghee Biscuits (Nei Biscuit; page 75) and Baked Coconut Barfi (page 56).

1 lb (454 g) unsalted butter, softened

Make the ghee. Roughly chop the butter and place it in a large, heavy-bottomed the pan, evenly covering the entire surface. Heat the pan over medium-low to medium heat, stirring occasionally when the butter begins to melt. When all the butter has melted, reduce the heat to the lowest setting and simmer gently. After about 1 minute, you will hear spluttering sounds from the bottom of the pan and see milk solids appearing on the surface.

Continue to simmer and stir occasionally until the color changes from pale yellow to light golden and the milk solids settle at the bottom. Simmer for 1 to 2 minutes, until medium- to large-sized bubbles form on the top and the entire mixture is bubbling.

Remove the pan from heat and let it sit on the countertop until all simmering stops and browned bits of milk solids appear at the bottom. Strain the ghee while still hot by pouring it through a strainer or cheesecloth placed on top of a large glass jar. Don't worry about the fine tiny bubbles on the top, they will disappear as the ghee gradually cools.

For best storage, store the ghee in a cool and dark spot in the pantry. Properly stored, it can last up to 1 year at room temperature.

Homemade Khova (Mawa)

♠ Makes about ½ cup (100 g) ♠

Khova, also known as mawa, is a popular dairy product used in Indian cuisine. It has a slightly sweet, nutty flavor, and it is used as a base ingredient in many Indian sweets, including gulab jamun, barfi and *peda*. It is made by simmering milk until it thickens into a fudge-like texture, which can take several hours and requires constant stirring to prevent scorching. A quicker version can be made at home using milk powder, cream and ghee in the microwave—which is both time efficient and easy. This book includes a few recipes that call for khova, and they can be made completely in the microwave. It adds a rich, authentic flavor to Indian desserts, and its versatility makes it a staple ingredient in any Indian baker's pantry.

½ cup (34 g) nonfat dry milk powder

½ tsp ghee (page 190 or store-bought)

¼ cup plus 2 tbsp (90 ml) heavy whipping cream

Make the khova in the microwave. To prepare the khova, use a whisk to combine the milk powder, ghee and heavy whipping cream in a large, microwave-safe bowl. Microwave on high in 30-second intervals, stirring every 30 seconds, until the mixture has dried up and formed a solid mass. This should take around 2 to 3 minutes. Once the khova is ready, allow it to cool completely before using. It stays fresh in the refrigerator for 4 to 5 days.

Homemade Cake Flour

♠ Makes 1 cup (120 g) ♠

Cake flour is a finely milled flour that is low in protein and commonly used in baking to achieve a light, tender texture in cakes, cupcakes and other baked goods. If you don't have cake flour on hand, you can easily make it at home using all-purpose flour and cornstarch. Keep in mind that the texture and rise of your baked goods may vary slightly from those made with store-bought cake flour, but this substitution is a great option when you're in a pinch or want to avoid a trip to the grocery store.

1 cup (125 g) all-purpose flour

2 tbsp (16 g) corn flour or cornstarch

Make the cake flour. Measure 1 level cup of flour and remove 2 tablespoons (16 g) of the flour. Place the cup of flour into a mixing bowl. Add 2 tablespoons (16 g) of cornstarch to the flour. Sift the flour and cornstarch until well combined. Use the mixture as a substitute for 1 cup (120 g) of cake flour in your recipe. This cake flour substitute will help to produce a lighter and more delicate texture in your baked goods, similar to the texture achieved with store-bought cake flour.

Acknowledgments

As we come to the end of this book, it's hard to believe that I've actually written it. Sometimes I have to pinch myself just to confirm that this accomplishment is real. It still feels surreal, and it has been an absolute pleasure to create this "new baby" of mine. This journey was filled with so many emotions, so much recipe testing and dreaming about how to present these desserts in a simple and approachable way for even the most novice of bakers. I strove to make each recipe as easy as possible for beginner bakers to follow, while still maintaining the delicious flavors and textures that make each dessert unique. This book is truly a labor of love, and I owe a debt of gratitude to so many people who have helped me along the way. A simple thank you would not be enough to express my appreciation.

First, I want to express my gratitude to my mother. Thank you so much, Amma. I am forever indebted to you.

To Page Street Publishing, without whom this book wouldn't have been possible. Thank you so much for making my dream a reality and I'll be forever grateful. A special thanks to my editor, Emily Archbold, for your guidance, support and expertise in bringing this book to life.

I would like to express my heartfelt gratitude to all my followers and supporters on Instagram and my blog. Your support and encouragement have been instrumental in making this dream of mine a reality. I am truly grateful and thank you for being a part of this journey with me.

To my husband, Rakesh, whose unwavering support and encouragement have been invaluable to me on this journey. You have played an integral role in shaping me into the person I am today, and I am forever indebted to you for that. Thank you

for trusting me and encouraging me to follow my dreams no matter what. Above all, I want to thank you for being my constant companion throughout the arduous nine months of recipe testing, and for your support during the inevitable emotional ups and downs that accompanied this project. I can never thank you enough for being my rock throughout this journey. I love you, Ji!

To my wonderful kids, Riaan and Kiara, for their unwavering support and assistance throughout this project. You have tasted every recipe in this book and provided invaluable feedback, always encouraging me with your kind words and expressions of admiration. Hearing you say "Mama, you are an amazing baker" fills me with an overwhelming sense of joy, emotion and pride. I feel incredibly blessed to have such wonderful children, and I am so thankful to God for you. Thank you, my dear Riaan and Kiara, for being my little helpers and my biggest fans.

To my family, without your support and motivation this would not have been possible. Thank you Mummy, Daddy, Paa and Maa for believing in me and always encouraging me to follow my dreams.

Finally, I would like to express my sincere gratitude to my dear friends Sruthi, Janani, Vineeth, Hari and Swaran. Your unwavering support and willingness to taste every dessert, no matter how many times I served them, and provision of honest feedback and critiques, played a crucial role in helping me perfect my recipes. Thank you for taking the time to test each recipe, for your invaluable support, motivation and encouragement, and for making every weekend a fun and memorable one. I am grateful to have you all in my life, and I couldn't have done this without you. Thank you from the bottom of my heart.

About the Author

Janani Elavazhagan is a self-taught baker, recipe developer, food stylist and photographer. She is the creator of the food blog *Skillet To Plate*. Known for her delicious recipes as well as her stunning photography, she also works as a stock food photographer for OFFSET and The Picture Pantry. She has developed recipes and photographed for top brands including Amoretti, Rodelle, Suncore Foods, Wüsthof, Erath Winery, Taylor & Colledge, Lifeway Foods and Roland Foods, among others. She loves creating and capturing beautiful food stories and sharing her vision of food with others. She currently lives in Portland, Oregon, with her better half, two children and fur babies, Chase and Skye.

INDEX